25 Lessons from Ted Lasso

Why Empathy and Optimism Are The Real Superpowers

Michael E. McGrath

September 16, 2025

Copyright © 2025 Michel E. McGrath. All rights reserved. No part of this publication may be reproduced without prior written permission from the author. For information, contact: michael_e_mcgrath@icloud.com

Cover created using AI (ChatGPT) with Apple TV+ promotional photos. There is no express or implied endorsement of this book.

Acknowledgment

I want to acknowledge the inspiration and source material for this book: the writers, producers, and lead actors of Ted Lasso.

Primary Writers:
- **Jason Sudeikis** – series co-creator, lead actor (Ted Lasso), and frequent writer.
- **Bill Lawrence** – co-creator,
- **Brendan Hunt** – co-creator, plays Coach Beard, and major contributor to writing.
- **Joe Kelly** – co-creator,

The writing staff across the seasons:
- **Brett Goldstein** – plays Roy Kent, joined as a writer before being cast, and wrote several standout episodes.
- **Phoebe Walsh** – wrote and co-wrote multiple episodes,
- **Leann Bowen** – writer on Season 1,

Main Cast
- Jason Sudeikis – Ted Lasso
- **Hannah Waddingham** – Rebecca Welton
- **Jeremy Swift** – Leslie Higgins
- **Phil Dunster** – Jamie Tartt
- Brett Goldstein – Roy Kent
- **Brendan Hunt** – Coach Beard
- **Nick Mohammed** – Nathan "Nate" Shelley
- **Juno Temple** – Keeley Jone

Executive Producers
- **Jason Sudeikis** – co-creator, star, and creative force.
- **Bill Lawrence** – co-creator, showrunner
- **Brendan Hunt** – co-creator, writer, and actor
- **Joe Kelly** – co-creator and writer.
- **Jeff Ingold** – executive producer
- **Liza Katzer** – executive producer
- **Bill Wrubel** – executive producer and writer.

Table of Contents

Introduction 1
Lesson #1: Be Curious, Not Judgmental 9
Lesson #2: The Strength of Admitting 'I Don't Know' 15
Lesson #3: Create, Don't Imitate 21
Lesson #4: Embrace the Gift of the Present 29
Lesson #5: The Power of Belief Beyond Symbols 37
Lesson #6: Create Your Own Luck 47
Lesson #7: Authentic Apologies and Acceptance 55
Lesson #8: Let Go and Move Forward 65
Lesson #9: Value Hard Lessons 73
Lesson #10: Don't Settle for "Fine" 81
Lesson #11: Transform Impossible into I'm Possible 87
Lesson #12: Find Strength in Shared Struggle 95
Lesson #13: Trust Your Moral Compass 103
Lesson #14: Stay Present and Take Action 111
Lesson #15: Your Choices Define You More 119
Lesson #16: Stop the Self-Criticism Symphony 127
Lesson #17: It's the Lack of Hope That Gets You 135
Lesson #18: Total Football is Life 145
Lesson #19: The Isaac Cut—Small Acts, Big Love 153
Lesson #20: It Will All Work Out 161
Lesson #21: The Gut-Heart Check-In 167
Lesson #22: Never Give Up on People 173
Lesson #23: Love Gets You Through 179
Lesson #24: Don't Fight Back. Fight Forward 185
Lesson #25: Leave Well 195
Conclusion: Choosing Empathy, Practicing Optimism 205

About the Author

Michael E. McGrath is an experienced management consultant, executive, and author of the following books:

Generative AI Series

Generative AI for Everyday Use (2025)

How Generative AI Can Transform Education (2025)

Decision Making & Leadership Series

25 Lessons from Ted Lasso: Why Empathy and Optimism Are the Real Superpowers (2025)

Decision Making: The Key to Success in Life and Business (2025)

The Wit and Wisdom of Decisions (2016 and 2025)

Decide Better for A Better Life (2008)

Business Decisions (2009)

Decide Better for College (2009)

Autonomous Vehicle Series

Autonomous Vehicles: Opportunities, Strategies, and Disruptions (Original 2018, 5th Edition 2025)

Beginner's Guide to Autonomous Vehicles (2019)

Product Strategy Series

Product Strategy for High Technology Companies (1995, Revised 2000)

Understanding and Applying Product Platform Strategy (2016)

Setting The PACE in Product Development (1996)

Product Development: Success Through PACE (1992)

Next Generation Product Development (2004)

He has a BS in Computer Science from Boston College, an MBA from Harvard Business School, and a Doctor of Letters (honoris causa) from St. Michael's College.

Introduction

In a time marked by cynicism, division, and the relentless chase for personal success at any cost, a mustachioed American football coach from Kansas quietly transformed our understanding of what it means to lead, to inspire, and to make meaningful change in the world. Ted Lasso didn't arrive at AFC Richmond with a playbook full of complex strategies or a resume packed with championship wins. Instead, he was armed with something much more powerful and scarce: a steadfast belief in the transformative strength of empathy and optimism.

When Ted Lasso premiered on Apple TV+ in 2020, the world was facing unprecedented challenges. A global pandemic had isolated us from each other, political divisions seemed insurmountable, and many people questioned whether kindness and compassion had any place in an increasingly harsh and competitive world. Into this landscape stepped Ted Lasso, a character who would prove that empathy and optimism are not just nice-to-have qualities or signs of naivety, but powerful forces capable of transforming individuals, teams, and entire communities.

Why the World Needed Ted Lasso
It seems absurd when you think about it: the world didn't need another gritty antihero or brooding mastermind. What we needed was someone who looked us in the eye and said, "I believe in you." Someone who showed that kindness isn't weakness, optimism isn't naivete, and empathy isn't optional. Ted Lasso wasn't just a character on Apple TV+; he was a cultural intervention that we needed at that time.

The Ted Lasso Story

I expect that most readers have already watched the show, but in case you haven't yet, or you need a refresher, here is the "readers' digest" version.

Ted Lasso begins with a daring idea: an American college football coach with no experience in English soccer is hired to lead AFC Richmond, a struggling Premier League team. The club's owner, Rebecca Welton, secretly hopes he will fail as part of a plan to get revenge on her unfaithful ex-husband, who used to own the team. But instead of being embarrassed, Ted wins everyone over with his endless optimism, folksy humor, and fresh-baked biscuits every morning. Season One shows Ted earning the trust of skeptics, including the sharp-tongued media, the cynical veteran Roy Kent, and the arrogant striker Jamie Tartt, by caring more about people than just winning. By the end of the season, Richmond faces relegation, but Ted has already changed the club's culture into something more substantial than the league standings.

Season Two deepens the story, showing that optimism doesn't mean life is easy. Ted faces panic attacks and begins therapy, revealing the emotional toll of his divorce and the challenges of leading while hurting. The season explores vulnerability and healing: Rebecca finds new love, Roy discovers purpose after retiring, and Jamie learns humility. Meanwhile, Nate the kit man is promoted to assistant coach, but his insecurities and hunger for recognition start to fester. Richmond earns promotion back to the Premier League, but Nate's growing resentment leads to betrayal, as he leaks Ted's panic attack to the press and storms out to join a rival club.

Season Three raises the stakes both on and off the field. Richmond is mocked as likely to finish last, especially under Nate's new leadership at West Ham, but the Greyhounds gradually find their rhythm. The introduction of "Total Football," a strategy based on trust, adaptability, and teamwork, reflects the personal growth of the players, who learn to rely on each other instead of playing as individuals. Rebecca struggles with her own purpose beyond revenge, Roy and Keeley navigate love and identity, and Jamie evolves from a self-centered star into a true team player. Ted's leadership is tested, but his faith in kindness and connection continues to transform lives.

By the finale, the show comes full circle. Nate seeks forgiveness and finds redemption. Richmond beats West Ham and comes within a hair of winning the league. Rebecca discovers peace in letting go of bitterness, Roy steps up into leadership, and Ted chooses to return home to Kansas to be with his son. His farewell is bittersweet but fitting: he leaves behind not just a better football club but better people. Across three seasons, *Ted Lasso* reminds us that empathy, optimism, and belief are not just slogans. They are transformative forces that can turn a group of misfits into a family and a football pitch into a classroom for life.

The show was expected to end at season three, but as I write this book, they are filming a new season four.

Empathy and Optimism:
Not Fluffy, But Fierce

Let's get this straight right away: empathy and optimism are not the soft, fluffy qualities reserved for greeting cards and motivational posters. They are, in fact, the fiercest forces of human progress.

Think about it. Empathy is what lets us step into another person's shoes, preferably not Nate's, since he tends to walk into metaphorical messes, and understand their struggles. Optimism is what gives us the courage to lace up our own shoes and take the next step, even when the road is rough.

Ted wielded these qualities like superpowers. He disarmed cynics with kindness, softened the hardest hearts with compassion, and rebuilt a fractured team not through strategy but through belief. Rebecca, the icy club owner who hired him to fail, thawed into someone capable of trust and vulnerability. Roy Kent, the human embodiment of a growl, rediscovered tenderness without losing his edge. Jamie Tartt, the diva striker, transformed into someone who could finally say the words, "I'm sorry."

This wasn't sentimentality; it was transformation. Empathy and optimism don't just change moods; they change lives.

Not Magic, Just Humanity

Here's the thing: Ted Lasso isn't magical. He's not sprinkling fairy dust over people's heads, making them suddenly enlightened. He's painfully human. He gets panic attacks. His marriage falls apart. He has days when his smile is forced, and his jokes fall flat.

That's the genius of Ted's example: optimism doesn't mean everything is fine. It means choosing to believe that things *can* improve, even when they aren't okay right now. Empathy doesn't mean excusing every mistake. It means refusing to let someone's worst behavior define them forever.

This is why Ted resonates. He's not some perfect guru floating above the chaos. He's knee-deep in the mud with us, cracking a joke, offering a hand, and saying, "Hey, let's figure this out together."

Lessons That Sneak Up on You

What makes *Ted Lasso* so brilliant is how its lessons sneak up on you. You come for the comedy, the fish-out-of-water coach who doesn't know offsides from an offside sandwich, but you stay because you realize you're learning how to be a better human.

Take the well-known dart game with Rupert. On the surface, it's a simple pub bet. But embedded in it is one of Ted's most important truths: "Be curious, not judgmental." That's not just good pub banter; it's a guiding life principle. Imagine how many conflicts could be avoided if people asked questions instead of jumping to conclusions. (Looking at you, social media warriors.)

Or think of the "BELIEVE" sign. It wasn't just tape and cardboard. It was a reminder that belief must live in us, not above us. When the sign tore, the belief didn't disappear because Ted had already planted it in people's hearts.

Even Roy's signature grunt is a lesson in disguise: sometimes words aren't needed. Presence speaks louder.

That's the beauty of the show: it offers life lessons wrapped in football metaphors, biscuits, and locker-room banter.

Why Leadership Is for Everyone

You might be thinking, "This is all useful, but I'm not a coach, a CEO, or even the captain of my bowling league. Why should I care about leadership lessons?"

Here's the answer: because you're leading, whether you realize it or not.

Parents guide their kids. Friends support friends through breakups, job searches, and bad hair days. Teachers manage classrooms. Colleagues run meetings.

Leadership isn't about job titles. It's about influence. Influence is something we all have. Every time you choose empathy over judgment, optimism over despair, or kindness over cruelty, you're leading. You're shaping the culture around you. You're coaching your own version of AFC Richmond, whether it's your family, your workplace, or your group of friends.

So don't think of this book as a leadership manual just for managers. Think of it as a life manual for anyone who wants to be a little more Ted and a little less Rupert.

The Ripple Effect of Kindness

One of the most powerful things Ted Lasso shows us is how small actions ripple outward in enormous ways.

A box of biscuits softens a bitter boss. An apology heals a fractured friendship. A moment of patience gives someone the courage to try again.

Ted wasn't handing out grand speeches every day. Most of the time, he was just showing up with presence, humor, and a refusal to give up on people. And that's what changed everything.

Kindness isn't weak. It's strategic. Optimism isn't foolish. It's resilient. Together, they're how revolutions of the heart begin.

And here's the kicker: you don't have to be Ted to start a ripple. You just have to do the small, kind thing in front of you. The rest takes care of itself.

A Preview of the 25 Lessons

Ted Lasso wasn't just a coach; he was a life teacher. The 25 lessons in this book aren't abstract ideas or leadership clichés: they're practical, heartfelt insights from Ted's journey and the journeys of those around him. Collectively, they serve as a playbook for living with empathy, optimism, and courage in a world that often seems to work against these qualities.

These lessons start with curiosity, which is the foundation of Ted's worldview. Instead of rushing to judgment, he demonstrates how to ask better questions, listen before deciding, and prioritize understanding over certainty. That simple shift in mindset, "Be curious, not judgmental," can change conflicts, workplaces, and relationships.

From there, the lessons focus on humility and growth. Ted demonstrated the power of admitting "I don't know" and the joy of creating rather than copying. He reminded us that success isn't about following someone else's path but about daring to write your own playbook.

We also learn about time and presence. In an age of distraction, Ted grounded himself and others in the gift of the present moment. Whether celebrating small wins or comforting someone in pain, he demonstrated that the here and now is where growth, connection, and healing happen.

Throughout the series, belief was a recurring theme, not just the yellow sign taped above a locker room door, but the deeper truth that belief must reside in people, not symbols. Lesson after lesson, Ted showed us that genuine belief can't be outsourced; it must be nurtured from within, fueled by optimism and reinforced through action.

Other lessons highlight resilience, creating your own luck when circumstances seem stacked against you, learning to let go and move forward when old stories no longer serve you, and valuing the hard lessons that come with discomfort and failure. Richmond's relegation, for instance, was more than a plot twist; it was a master class in how setbacks can build character, deepen trust, and bolster resolve.

Ted's approach also highlighted emotional intelligence. He taught the art of genuine apologies and empathy in acceptance, the ability to turn "impossible" into "I'm possible," and the strength that comes from shared struggles. These lessons remind us that leadership isn't about exerting power over others but about building connections with others.

Equally important are lessons about identity and choice: that your moral compass must guide your actions, that presence requires courage, and that your choices define you far more than your talents ever will. Ted demonstrated how to stop the endless "self-criticism symphony" and replace it with hope, humor, and honest self-compassion.

The second half of the book shines a light on teamwork, love, and legacy. We discover that "Total Football" isn't just a strategy. It's a metaphor for life: we succeed when we flex, adapt, and cover for each other. The "Isaac Cut" reminds us how small acts of kindness ripple outward into powerful transformations. We learn to trust the process even when chaos seems to reign, to check in with our gut and heart as our internal GPS, and above all, to never give up on people, even when they've given up on themselves.

Ted's final lessons show us the sustaining power of love—love as the ultimate problem solver, love as the fuel that carries us through despair, and love as the essence of optimism itself. The show taught us not to fight back but to fight forward, channeling struggle into growth, and, when the time comes, to "leave well"—to exit relationships, jobs, or chapters of life with grace, gratitude, and a blessing for what's ahead.

Together, these 25 lessons are more than just a list. They are a tapestry of wisdom about living with empathy and optimism, not as lofty ideals but as daily habits. They challenge us to see setbacks as opportunities for growth, to treat people beyond their roles, and to believe in ourselves, in others, and in the promise of a better tomorrow.

Readers will find themselves nodding, laughing, tearing up, and most of all, inspired to put these lessons into action. Because at the end of the day, Ted didn't just teach us how to win on the pitch. He taught us how to win at life by becoming, in his words, "better humans."

The Journey Ahead

This book captures the wisdom of Ted Lasso's three seasons and condenses it into 25 lessons. But don't worry, this isn't a dry list of "dos and don'ts." These lessons are lively, ongoing reminders that life isn't about perfection but about progress.

You'll learn why curiosity trumps judgment, why vulnerability is strength, why hope beats fear, and why sometimes the most courageous thing you can do is walk away gracefully. And you'll be challenged to apply these lessons not by becoming Ted, but by becoming the best version of yourself.

I learned a great deal while writing this book. My traditional leadership style was authoritative and decisive, with an emphasis on accountability, discipline, control, and toughness. As I worked my way through these lessons, I learned that there is hidden value in empathy and optimism.

By the end, you won't just know the lessons. You'll feel them. You'll carry them.

Lesson #1:
Be Curious, Not Judgmental

The Example:

Ted's quote: "*Be curious, not judgmental.*"

--- Ted Lasso (via Walt Whitman, in the dart match scene from Season 1, Episode 8: "The Diamond Dogs")

I start this book with what might be the most important lesson for today's world. What if we all used curiosity to learn more about each other, especially those we disagree with? Instead of Facebook criticisms, extremist rants on X, arguments with friends and family, and political divisions, we tried to understand each other: curiosity instead of judgment.

In one of the most pivotal moments of Ted Lasso's first season, we find ourselves in the Crown & Anchor pub where Ted faces off against Rupert Mannion, Rebecca's manipulative ex-husband, in what appears to be a friendly game of darts. Throughout the series, Ted has been repeatedly underestimated. He was perceived as the bumbling American who doesn't understand football, is too nice for his own good, and surely can't compete in the cutthroat world of English Premier League soccer.

Context
Here's the context:

- Ted challenges Rupert (Rebecca's ex-husband) to a high-stakes darts game at The Crown & Anchor pub.
- Everyone assumes Ted will lose, but during the match, Ted reflects on how people have constantly underestimated him.

- He explains that over the years, many judged him without ever asking questions, like whether he'd played darts before.
- That's when he drops the quote: "Guys have underestimated me my entire life. And it used to really bother me. But then one day, I was driving my little boy to school, and I saw a quote by Walt Whitman. It said, 'Be curious, not judgmental.'"
- Ted then reveals that he's been playing darts every Sunday with his father since he was a kid and proceeds to win the match with style.

It's one of the show's most iconic scenes.

Rupert, embodying the smug superiority Ted faces every day, wagers that Ted will embarrass himself at darts. The pub falls silent as everyone expects to see yet another display of American incompetence. But then Ted steps up, says those six transformative words, and hits a perfect bullseye: "Be curious, not judgmental."

What makes this moment so powerful isn't just Ted's unexpected skill. He shows that people underestimated him because they judged him without curiosity. They saw his Kansas accent, his folksy sayings, and his relentless optimism and stopped paying attention. They never asked why this man was chosen to coach an elite team, nor wondered what depth might hide beneath his surface-level friendliness.

Interestingly, although the quote has been widely misattributed to Whitman, it doesn't appear in any of his writings. Whitman scholars have confirmed it's not his. In fact, the line first appeared much later, in the 20th century, but without a clear original source. It seems to have circulated as an inspirational quote, and Ted Lasso made it popular by linking it to Whitman. So, while it's a great piece of wisdom that fits Ted's outlook, it's not actually Whitman's line. However, it's actually a paraphrase of the poet's broader idea about approaching others with curiosity instead of judgment.

The scene serves as a masterclass in the influence of being underestimated and the risk of jumping to conclusions. In that moment, Ted doesn't just win a game of darts; he gains respect, transforms the room's atmosphere, and shows that wisdom often comes in unexpected forms.

Explanation

When Ted delivers this line during the darts match, it's more than a clever comeback; it's a life philosophy that questions one of humanity's most harmful tendencies. Too often, we rush to label people without taking the time to understand them. We often assume we know their story, skills, or intentions based on superficial observations, such as their appearance, accent, job title, or first impression.

This rush to judgment isn't entirely our fault. Our brains are evolutionarily wired to make quick assessments for survival purposes. In prehistoric times, rapidly determining friend from foe could mean the difference between life and death. But in our modern, complex world, this ancient programming often does more harm than good, causing us to miss opportunities, misunderstand people, and perpetuate harmful stereotypes.

Ted flips that idea around with simple elegance. Instead of judging, he chooses curiosity. Instead of dismissing someone, he regularly seeks to understand them. Instead of assuming he knows the whole story, he asks questions that bring new insights. That core shift in approach changes everything about how we navigate the world and how others perceive us.

Curiosity builds bridges where judgment creates walls. It opens doors to empathy, learning, and deeper connections that might otherwise remain closed forever. When we approach someone with genuine curiosity, we demonstrate that they matter, that their experience is valuable, and that they deserve to be seen and understood, rather than merely being categorized and dismissed.

Judgment, on the other hand, damages relationships. When we judge first, we shut ourselves off from possibilities and people who could surprise us, teach us, or become vital parts of our lives. We restrict not only our understanding of others but also our own potential for growth and connection.

Reflect on the stark difference between thinking "That person is weird" and considering, "I wonder what experiences shaped their unique perspective." One attitude dismisses the person, while the other invites curiosity. The first attitude creates distance; the second encourages connection. The first limits us, but the second helps us grow.

Application

To apply this lesson, try this four-step practice the next time you feel yourself judging someone, whether it's a colleague, family member, stranger, or even yourself:

1. **Pause and Notice:** Recognize the judgmental thought in real time ("He's lazy," "She's difficult," "They don't belong here," "I'm not good enough"). Awareness is the first step to change. Notice not only the thought but also the feeling that accompanies it. Often, there's a subtle sense of superiority, frustration, or dismissal.

2. **Ask with Genuine Interest:** Replace judgment with a curious question that assumes positive intent: "I wonder what's going on for them today?" "What might I not be seeing?" "What experiences might have led to this behavior?" "What could I learn from their perspective?" The key is to ask these questions with genuine interest, not sarcasm or disguised judgment.

3. **Connect and Investigate:** Find one small detail that helps you understand them better. This may involve having a real conversation, observing their actions more closely, or pausing to think about their possible circumstances. Look for the humanity behind the behavior: the smile that shows kindness, the shared struggle that creates common ground, the hidden talent or wisdom that wasn't immediately visible.

4. **Reflect and Integrate:** After gathering new information, consider what you learned and how it changed your initial assessment. Observe how your feelings about the person now differ from your first impression. This reflection helps

reinforce the importance of curiosity and increases the likelihood that you'll choose this approach again.

This shift demands intentional practice and self-kindness. You won't succeed every time, and that's okay. The aim isn't perfection, but progress, gradually rewiring your default response from judgment to curiosity. The rewards are life-changing: curiosity transforms strangers into friends, foes into allies, difficult coworkers into understood individuals, and ongoing challenges into chances for growth and learning.

Start small. Practice with low-pressure interactions: the grumpy-looking barista, the neighbor who keeps to themselves, the coworker whose methods differ from yours. As you build this curiosity muscle, you'll find it easier to extend the same patience to more challenging relationships and situations.

Takeaway

Every time you choose curiosity over judgment, you become a little wiser and much kinder. But more than that, you create space for others to be their authentic selves, demonstrate a better way of being human, and open yourself up to connections and insights that might otherwise pass you by.

In our world today that often feels divided and polarized, choosing curiosity over judgment isn't just a personal growth practice; it's an act of healing. It's how we begin to see each other as complex, worthy human beings instead of oversimplified categories or opponents.

The next time you're tempted to dismiss someone, remember Ted's wisdom: Be curious, not judgmental. You might discover that the person you're about to overlook has exactly what you need to learn, is facing struggles you never imagined, or possesses gifts that could enrich your life in unexpected ways.

Wouldn't the world be much less divisive if we used curiosity first to understand our differences instead of jumping to judgement?

Lesson #2:
The Strength of Admitting 'I Don't Know'

The Example:

> Ted's quote: "*You could fill two internets with what I don't know about football.*"

--- Ted Lasso (Season 1, Episode 1: "Pilot")

Traditionally, leaders were encouraged to project confidence in their expertise; however, Ted Lasso turned this around. In his very first press conference as the manager of AFC Richmond, facing a room full of skeptical British journalists who are clearly expecting him to fail, Ted delivers one of the most disarming lines in television: "You could fill two internets with what I don't know about football." In that moment, he does something that catches everyone completely off guard. He leads with his limitations rather than his strengths, his questions rather than his answers, and his curiosity rather than his expertise.

Context

Here's the context for the "two internets" example:

- The quote comes from Ted Lasso's very first press conference as manager of AFC Richmond, where he surprises skeptical journalists by openly admitting how much he doesn't know about football.
- Instead of projecting false confidence, Ted uses vulnerability and hum**or** to disarm hostility and establish authenticity.

- The line highlights intellectual humility, acknowledging the vastness of what he doesn't know while showing eagerness to learn.
- This moment sets the tone for his leadership style, one built on curiosity, growth, and connection rather than on maintaining the illusion of expertise.

This statement is groundbreaking because it breaks every rule of traditional leadership strategy. Typical advice suggests projecting confidence, emphasizing your credentials, and never showing weakness, especially in a hostile setting where others look for reasons to dismiss you. But Ted takes a different route, and by doing so, he turns what could have been a defensive, confrontational press conference into something entirely different.

The beauty of this admission lies not just in its honesty but in its accuracy. Ted doesn't say he knows nothing about football. He admits that there's a lot he doesn't understand, which ironically shows that he knows enough to see the extent of his ignorance. This is a mark of wisdom, not incompetence. He's basically saying, "I realize that this game is complicated enough that I need to stay humble about how much I still have to learn."

The phrase "two internets" is perfectly Ted—folksy, slightly absurd, but strangely accurate in capturing the scale of what he's discussing. It's both funny and modest, making his admission seem charming rather than worrying. He's not stuck in self-doubt; he's happily acknowledging reality while suggesting he's eager to learn more.

What makes this moment so pivotal is that it immediately establishes Ted's authenticity. In a room full of people expecting polish, pretense, or defensiveness, he offers genuine vulnerability. This creates an unexpected connection with his audience because vulnerability, when provided without shame or manipulation, tends to disarm hostility and create space for real human connection.

The quote also establishes Ted's learning-focused leadership style from the very beginning. By admitting what he doesn't know, he's not positioning himself as the guy with all the answers, but as the guy who's genuinely curious about finding them. This sets up a dynamic where learning, growth, and evolution become central to his leadership approach rather than needing to maintain the illusion of omniscience.

Explanation

Ted's willingness to admit the extent of his ignorance signifies a fundamental shift in how we view leadership, expertise, and credibility. In our culture, we're often told that admitting what we don't know shows weakness, that leaders should project confidence and certainty even when they are unsure. But Ted demonstrates that the opposite can be true, acknowledging our limitations can actually become a source of strength, connection, and effectiveness.

This approach works well because it's based on intellectual humility, a trait that research has shown to be one of the most valuable for learning, leadership, and relationship building. When we can honestly assess what we don't know, we become better at identifying what we need to learn, seeking help from others, and making decisions based on accurate rather than inflated views of our abilities.

Ted's admission also fosters psychological safety for everyone around him. When a leader is comfortable saying "I don't know," it allows others to acknowledge their own uncertainties, ask questions they might otherwise hesitate to voice, and share knowledge without fear of making the leader look bad. This creates a space where collective intelligence can thrive because everyone's expertise can be brought to bear rather than kept hidden.

The "two internets" line highlights an essential aspect of effective communication: sometimes the best way to convey a serious point is through gentle humor and surprising metaphors. Ted could have said, "There's a lot I don't know about football," but that would have been forgettable. The image of filling two internets with his ignorance is so vivid and funny that it sticks in people's minds while still getting across the key message about his humility and eagerness to learn.

This approach also reframes the relationship between knowledge and authority. Traditional models suggest that authority stems from knowing more than others. Still, Ted demonstrates that authority can also arise from being honest about what you don't know, while showing a genuine commitment to learning. People tend to trust leaders who are transparent about their limitations more than those who pretend to have expertise they don't possess.

Ted's admission is effective because it's paired with clear competence elsewhere. He might not understand football tactics, but he knows how to connect with others, communicate well, and foster positive team dynamics. By honestly admitting his lack of football knowledge, he actually emphasizes his strengths in human leadership without needing to state them outright.

The quote also establishes a growth mindset from the very beginning. By framing his ignorance as something that can be filled (like filling up the internet with information), Ted implies that not knowing something is temporary and addressable. He's not defining himself by his current limitations but by his potential for growth and learning.

Perhaps most importantly, this line shows that vulnerability can be a strategic choice rather than an unintentional exposure. Ted isn't unintentionally revealing weakness; he's intentionally choosing to be transparent because he knows this approach will ultimately benefit him and his team more than defensive posturing would.

Application

Learning to lead with intellectual humility like Ted requires both courage and strategy. Here's how to apply this approach in your own professional and personal contexts:

1. **Audit Your Knowledge Honestly:** Before entering new situations or taking on new responsibilities, do an honest assessment of what you know and what you don't know. This isn't about undermining your confidence, but about getting clear on where you need support, additional learning, or collaboration with others.

2. **Practice Strategic Vulnerability:** Like Ted, choose moments to admit what you don't know, especially when doing so can

build trust and create psychological safety for others. This works best when you couple admissions of ignorance with demonstrations of other competencies and clear commitments to learning.

3. **Reframe "I Don't Know" as "I Don't Know Yet":** When you encounter gaps in your knowledge, add the word "yet" to your internal dialogue. This simple addition transforms a fixed state into a growth opportunity and maintains your confidence while acknowledging current limitations. Share this approach with others to help create a learning culture around you.

4. **Use Humor to Soften Admissions:** Ted's "two internets" line works partly because it's genuinely funny. Develop your own style of making light of your limitations without minimizing them. This helps others feel comfortable with their own knowledge gaps and creates a more relaxed environment for learning and collaboration.

Takeaway

Ted's "two internets" line shows that intellectual humility isn't just a good personal trait. It's a strong leadership tactic that builds trust, creates psychological safety, and supports growth for individuals and groups. In a world that often praises pretending to know more than you do, being open about your limits can be a bold move that changes relationships and results.

This approach works because it is fundamentally more sustainable than trying to maintain facades of all-knowingness. When we're honest about what we don't know, we can focus our energy on truly learning instead of managing impressions. We can build authentic relationships based on mutual support and shared growth rather than on competitive positioning and defensive maneuvers.

Ted's willingness to admit his football ignorance also reveals something important about confidence. True confidence doesn't require knowing everything; it requires understanding yourself well and trusting your ability to learn. When we honestly assess our current skills and believe in our potential to improve, we become much better at facing new challenges and connecting with others.

The "two internets" line works because it blends humility with humor, uncertainty with optimism, and self-awareness with curiosity. It demonstrates that we don't have to choose between being honest about our limitations and being confident in our abilities. We can admit what we don't know while still showing competence, seek help while providing leadership, and stay learners while contributing.

The next time you're in a situation where you feel pressure to seem more knowledgeable than you are, remember Ted's example. Ask yourself: "How might transparency about my limitations actually strengthen my credibility and effectiveness?" Often, the answer is that people trust and follow leaders who are confident enough to be honest about their humanity, curious enough to keep learning, and wise enough to understand that admitting ignorance is often the first step toward genuine expertise.

Ultimately, Ted's "two internets" demonstrate that knowledge gaps aren't character flaws: they're opportunities to learn. And leaders who admit those gaps with humor, humility, and genuine curiosity often find that being authentic about what they don't know makes them more effective than those pretending to have all the answers.

You don't know everything, you may not even know as much as you need to know, but can you admit it?

Lesson #3:
Create, Don't Imitate

The Example:

Ted's philosophy: "*Be the best version of you, not someone else.*"

--- Expressed most clearly in Season 1, Episode 3 ("Trent Crimm: The Independent")

Ted Lasso's philosophy about "being the best version of you, not someone else" is most clearly expressed in Season 1, Episode 3 ("Trent Crimm: The Independent"). In this episode, Ted tells his team, especially Jamie Tartt, that success involves helping each person become their best self, both on and off the field.

Context
Here's the context:
- Ted says, "For me, success is not about the wins and losses. It's about helping these young fellas be the best versions of themselves on and off the field," reinforcing the importance of individuality, growth, and personal development.
- This message permeates the series, but this specific episode highlights Ted encouraging Jamie and the team to focus on themselves, supporting the spirit of "be the best version of you, not someone else" as a central lesson.
- Ted Lasso's encouragement for people to embrace and improve themselves, rather than imitate others, is delivered directly in Season 1, Episode 3, and echoed throughout the series.

- Ted consistently encourages players to develop their own strengths rather than copying others.
- He celebrates individual quirks and unique approaches rather than demanding conformity.
- When players try to imitate successful players or adopt personas that don't fit them, Ted gently guides them back to authenticity.
- The show repeatedly demonstrates that lasting success comes from authentic self-expression, not imitation.
- Characters who try to be someone else consistently struggle until they find their own voice.
- The most powerful transformations happen when characters stop performing and start being genuine.

This philosophy is most clearly shown through the character changes we see in the first three seasons, each representing a move from imitation to genuine self-expression.

Jamie Tartt's Evolution from Copycat to Original

Jamie's journey offers a clear example of moving from imitation to authenticity. When we first meet him, Jamie is essentially a mix of football's biggest egos—channeling Cristiano Ronaldo's arrogance, David Beckham's celebrity-seeking behavior, and Jack Grealish's flashy style. He's acting out what he thinks a star footballer should be rather than discovering who he truly is.

His transformation becomes most evident in Season 2 when he begins to strip away the performative aspects of his personality. The most pivotal moment comes in Season 2, Episode 8 ("Man City"), when Jamie breaks down after confronting his abusive father. In this scene, Roy Kent, who could have easily tried to mold Jamie into a version of himself, instead allows Jamie to be vulnerable and authentic, perhaps for the first time in his life.

By Season 3, Jamie has learned to channel his natural talent and charisma in ways that serve both him and his team, rather than simply imitating the behaviors of other football superstars. His playing style becomes uniquely his own, blending technical skill with genuine team spirit, something that can't be copied because it comes from his authentic self.

Nathan Shelley's Journey from Invisible to Individual

Nate's transformation is a strong example of choosing authenticity over imitation. At first, he's almost invisible: the "practice cone" of AFC Richmond, who is often bullied and ignored. When Ted first remembers his name and shows him respect, it marks the start of Nate's journey to find his own voice and sense of worth.

The dangerous shift in Nate's story occurs when he starts copying what he believes powerful coaches should be, becoming manipulative, cruel, and egotistical like the coaches he's observed from a distance. His Season 2 heel turn reveals what happens when someone attempts to succeed by mirroring toxic behaviors instead of leveraging their genuine strengths.

His redemption arc in Season 3 shows him learning to lead from his authentic strengths—his tactical intelligence, his deep love of the game, and his ability to grow, rather than trying to imitate the "special one" persona he believed he needed.

Roy Kent's Authentic Leadership Style

Roy's character, inspired by Roy Keane's intensity, exemplifies what genuine leadership looks like when someone stops trying to perform merely and instead leads from their true self. Throughout the series, Roy learns to combine his natural intensity with genuine care for others, creating a leadership style that's uniquely his own rather than copying traditional "hard man" coaching methods.

His relationship with Jamie becomes especially strong because Roy doesn't try to turn Jamie into a mini-Roy; instead, he helps Jamie find his own genuine way of being a leader and teammate.

Ted's Consistent Authenticity

Ted embodies this principle by staying "authentic to a fault, genuine in the face of criticism and failure, and true to himself at every turn." His leadership style is "all his own" rather than copying successful coaches he's studied. Even when pressured to change his approach or adopt more conventional tactics, Ted stays committed to his authentic way of coaching and living.

The series suggests that imitation might get you started, but creation, becoming the fullest, most authentic version of yourself, is what allows you to flourish truly. Ted's gift is seeing people not as they are or as they think they should be, but as they could become if they dared to be completely themselves.

Explanation

The tendency to imitate rather than create is one of humanity's most understandable yet limiting impulses. From childhood, we learn by watching and copying others. We observe successful people and try to replicate their behaviors, adopt their strategies, and even mirror their personalities. This imitative approach can be helpful for learning basics, but it becomes problematic when it prevents us from discovering and developing our own authentic gifts.

The main problem with imitation as a long-term plan is that it's always based on someone else's ideas. No matter how well you copy someone else, you're still following their plan instead of your own. You're trying to be the best version of someone else rather than the only version of yourself. This way of doing things has many built-in limits that stop us from reaching our true potential.

First, imitation depends on constant external references. When you're copying someone else's approach, you're constantly measuring yourself against their standards instead of developing your own internal guidance. This creates a dependency where your sense of success and direction relies on studying and copying your model rather than trusting your own instincts and judgment.

Second, imitation rarely considers the unique mix of circumstances, personality traits, experiences, and natural talents that make you truly you. What works perfectly for one person might be completely wrong for another, not because it's a poor strategy, but because it doesn't match their authentic strengths and natural way of being in the world.

Third, the world already has someone like the person you're trying to imitate. What it lacks is the unique contribution only you can offer. When you put your energy into copying someone else, you prevent the world from seeing the first-rate version of yourself that could emerge if you had the courage to create instead of imitate.

The "create, don't imitate" philosophy doesn't mean rejecting all influence or refusing to learn from others. Instead, it involves using external examples as inspiration and learning tools while trusting yourself to blend what you learn into something that is truly yours. It's the difference between copying someone else's painting and mastering techniques that help you express your own unique vision.

This approach takes much more courage than imitation because it involves exploring uncharted territory. When you copy someone, you have a clear roadmap and examples of success. When you forge your own path, you must trust that your authentic self has value, even if it doesn't resemble existing models of success.

The psychological concept of "imposter syndrome" often stems from this imitative mindset. When we're constantly trying to be someone else, we naturally feel like frauds because we're not being genuine. The cure isn't better imitation; it's finding the courage to show up as ourselves and trust that our authentic contribution has value.

Creating rather than imitating also allows for innovation and adaptation in ways that copying cannot. When you understand the principles behind why something works rather than just copying the surface behaviors, you can adapt those principles to new situations and combine them with your own insights to create something genuinely novel and compelling.

Perhaps most importantly, authentic creation is sustainable in ways that imitation isn't. When you're being yourself, you draw from an endless well of genuine motivation, natural energy, and intrinsic satisfaction. When you're copying someone else, you're constantly fighting against your own nature, which is exhausting and ultimately unsustainable.

Application

Try this expanded four-step practice to help yourself move from imitation to authentic creation:

1. **Identify Your Imitation Patterns:** Take an honest inventory of where you might be copying others rather than developing

your own authentic approach. Ask yourself: In what areas am I trying to be like someone else? What aspects of my work style, leadership approach, creative expression, or even personal relationships are based on imitating role models rather than expressing my authentic self?

2. **Discover Your Authentic Talents:** Identify the unique combination of traits, experiences, values, and natural talents that make you distinctively you. These are the raw materials from which you can create something original. These unique elements are the foundation from which you can create rather than imitate.

3. **Experiment with Authentic Expression:** Choose one area where you've been imitating others and experiment with expressing your authentic self instead. Start small and pay attention to how it feels different to create from authenticity versus copying from imitation.

4. **Expand Your Unique Self:** Gradually expand your capacity for authentic creation by regularly practicing original thinking and expression. The goal is to strengthen your confidence in your own creative capacity and your trust in the value of your authentic perspective.

Remember that shifting from imitation to creation is a gradual process, not an instant change. You will probably oscillate between copying and creating as you develop confidence in your own voice and style. The important thing is to steadily increase the amount of your work that is genuinely original, rather than heavily influenced by outside sources.

Also recognize that learning from others and being influenced by them is a natural and valuable process. The goal isn't to isolate yourself from all external input. The key difference is whether you're using external examples as springboards for your own creative growth or as templates to copy exactly. Healthy influence passes through you and is shaped by your unique perspective; unhealthy imitation tries to replace your view with someone else's.

Most importantly, trust that your true self has something valuable to offer. The reason you're attracted to certain role models isn't because you should become like them, but because you recognize something in them that resonates with undeveloped parts of your own potential. Your task is to nurture that potential in your own way, not to become a copy of the person who first showed you it was possible.

Takeaway

Whenever you choose to create from your authentic self rather than imitate someone else's success, you contribute something to the world that has never existed before and will never exist again. You also allow others to do the same, fostering a culture where originality is valued over conformity.

The world doesn't need another copy of someone who already exists, no matter how successful or admirable that person might be. What it truly needs is the first and only version of you, fully expressed and confidently shared. Your unique combination of traits, experiences, and perspectives could be exactly what someone else needs to see, learn from, or be inspired by.

The next time you find yourself trying to be like someone else, remember that imitation might feel safer, but creation is where the magic happens. Ask yourself: "What would I contribute if I trusted that being myself was enough?" "How would I approach this challenge if I couldn't copy anyone else's method?" "What would I create if I believed my authentic voice had value?"

After all, as every character transformation in Ted Lasso shows, the most impressive results come not from copying someone else, but from becoming a more whole and confident version of yourself. The world already has plenty of copies. What it's waiting for is your original voice.

Lesson #4:
Embrace the Gift of the Present

The Example:

> Ted's quote: "*Living in the moment, it's a gift. That's why they call it the present.*"
>
> --- Ted Lasso, Season 2, Episode 7: "Headspace"

This thoughtful wordplay comes during "Headspace," an episode that focuses heavily on mental health, psychological well-being, and the importance of being present rather than trapped by past regrets or future anxieties. The timing is significant. Season 2, Episode 7 occurs during a period when multiple characters are struggling with psychological challenges that pull them away from present-moment awareness.

Context

Here is the contextual background and reason for Ted Lasso's quote:

- Ted Lasso delivers this line during a time when both he and several key AFC Richmond characters are struggling with anxiety, overthinking, and avoidance.
- The team and coaching staff are dealing with conflict, personal challenges, and self-doubt. Ted himself is in therapy, struggling to address unresolved feelings about his marriage and leadership.
- The quote is offered as warm advice to focus on mindfulness: appreciating the present

- Ted senses that everyone, including himself, needs to stop fixating on regrets (past) or fears (future) to find happiness and clarity.
- He's encouraging his team (and himself) to embrace the current moment as an opportunity for growth, healing, and connection.
- The statement helps reframe struggle and uncertainty as a chance to move forward, emphasizing the power of gratitude and presence.

The quote echoes the show's broader theme of vulnerability, self-acceptance, and finding meaning even in adversity. Ted's lesson is both personal and universal, offering comfort and hope to characters and viewers facing tough times, transitions, or emotional overwhelm. This context shows how Ted draws on wisdom and empathy to empower others to live fully, reminding everyone that the greatest value is often found in the present moment.

The quote represents more than clever wordplay; it embodies a fundamental principle of psychological well-being that appears throughout mindfulness traditions, positive psychology, and therapeutic approaches. Ted's observation about the "present" being a "gift" captures the profound truth that our capacity for happiness, effectiveness, and genuine connection exists primarily in the current moment rather than in our memories of the past or fantasies about the future.

The Context of Season 2's Mental Health Focus
By Episode 7 of Season 2, the series has introduced Dr. Sharon Fieldstone, the sports psychologist, and begun exploring mental health themes more explicitly. Ted is struggling with his resistance to therapy while simultaneously experiencing panic attacks that force him to confront his psychological patterns. Other characters are also facing challenges that require them to be more present and aware rather than operating on autopilot or being consumed by past traumas or future fears.

The episode deals with various characters learning to pay attention to their current experiences rather than being hijacked by automatic reactions, old wounds, or anticipatory anxiety. In this context, Ted's reminder about the gift of the present moment serves as both personal insight and coaching philosophy, a way of helping himself and others find stability and clarity amid psychological turbulence.

Ted's delivery of this line reflects someone who is learning to apply mindfulness principles not just as abstract concepts but as practical tools for navigating real psychological challenges. This isn't Ted speaking from a place of easy optimism but from someone who is discovering the necessity of present-moment awareness for mental health and well-being.

The Psychological Science of Present-Moment Awareness

Ted's wordplay aligns with decades of research in psychology and neuroscience about the benefits of present-moment awareness. Studies consistently show that people who can maintain their attention on the present experience, rather than being lost in regretful thoughts about the past or anxious thoughts about the future, report higher levels of happiness, lower levels of stress, and better overall mental health.

This is particularly relevant for the high-pressure environment of professional sports, where athletes often struggle with performance anxiety (future-focused worry) or dwelling on past mistakes. Ted's philosophy about living in the present moment offers both a performance strategy and a mental health practice.

Applications Throughout the Episode and Series

In "Headspace," we see various characters learning to apply present-moment awareness in different ways. The episode explores how being present can help with emotional regulation, decision-making, and interpersonal connections. Characters who can stay grounded in the current moment tend to respond more effectively to challenges than those who are lost in mental time travel.

Ted's own journey with panic attacks becomes an opportunity to practice present-moment awareness. Rather than being consumed by fears about future panic attacks or shame about past episodes, Ted gradually learns to stay present with his current experience and seek appropriate help for his mental health.

The episode also shows how present-moment awareness affects athletic performance. Players who can stay focused on the current play, current opportunity, or current moment tend to perform better than those who are mentally replaying past mistakes or worrying about future outcomes.

The Balance Between Present-Focus and Planning

One of the sophisticated aspects of Ted's philosophy is that it doesn't advocate for completely ignoring the past or future. Learning from past experiences and planning for future challenges are important life skills. The key insight is about where we place our primary attention and emotional energy.

The "present as gift" concept suggests that while we can briefly visit the past for learning or the future for planning, our home base should be the current moment, where we truly have agency, where relationships truly happen, and where life truly unfolds.

Throughout the series, Ted demonstrates this balance. He reflects on past experiences when there are lessons to extract, and he plans for future matches and challenges, but he doesn't get trapped in regret about what's already happened or anxiety about what might happen. His primary focus remains on what he can do and experience in the present.

Season 3 and the Maturation of Present-Moment Living

By Season 3, we see how various characters have internalized the practice of present-moment awareness. They've learned to catch themselves when their minds drift into unproductive past-focused regret or future-focused anxiety, and they've developed skills for redirecting their attention to the present moment, where they can take effective action.

The series finale demonstrates the fruition of this philosophy as characters make important decisions based on present-moment clarity rather than being driven by past patterns or future fears. They've learned to treat each moment as a gift that deserves their full attention and appreciation.

A summary across multiple episodes and seasons illustrates this concept:

- Ted introduces present-moment awareness as both a performance tool and a mental health practice
- The philosophy helps characters manage anxiety, regret, and other forms of psychological suffering
- Present-moment living improves both athletic performance and interpersonal relationships
- Characters learn to balance present focus with appropriate learning from the past and planning for the future
- The practice becomes particularly important for managing high-pressure situations and mental health challenges
- By Season 3, present-moment awareness has become integrated into the team culture and individual character development
- The series demonstrates how mindfulness practices can be practical tools rather than abstract concepts

Explanation

The capacity to live fully in the present moment represents one of the most fundamental yet challenging aspects of human well-being and effectiveness. Even though the present moment is the only time when life actually occurs—when we can take action, experience joy, connect with others, or influence outcomes—most people spend most of their mental energy focused on the past or future.

This tendency toward mental time travel isn't inherently problematic. Our ability to learn from past experiences and plan for future challenges has evolutionary advantages and practical benefits. The issue arises when we become trapped in unproductive forms of past or future thinking—ruminating about things we cannot change, rehearsing conversations that may never happen, or creating anxiety about outcomes we cannot control.

Research in psychology shows that excessive focus on the past often leads to depression (particularly when focused on regrets, losses, or traumatic experiences), while excessive focus on the future often leads to anxiety (particularly when focused on potential threats, failures, or uncertainties). Present-moment awareness offers a refuge from both forms of psychological suffering.

The "present as gift" metaphor is particularly powerful because it reframes our relationship with time from scarcity to abundance. When we're focused on what we've lost or what we might lose, time feels scarce and precious in a way that creates pressure and anxiety. When we recognize each moment as a gift to be received and appreciated, we access a sense of abundance and gratitude that supports both well-being and effectiveness.

Present-moment awareness also enhances our capacity for what psychologists call "flow states"—periods of optimal performance and satisfaction where we become fully absorbed in our current activity. These states are only accessible when our attention is unified and focused on what we're doing right now, rather than being divided between the current activity and mental commentary about the past or future.

Additionally, authentic relationships and genuine intimacy only occur in the present moment. While we can share memories of the past or dreams for the future, actual connection happens through present-moment attention to ourselves and others. When we're mentally elsewhere during conversations or interactions, we miss the subtle cues, emotional nuances, and opportunities for deeper connection that are available right now.

The practice of present-moment living also increases our sense of agency and empowerment. The past is already fixed and cannot be changed, while the future hasn't happened yet and may unfold in unpredictable ways. The present moment is where our actual influence exists—where we can make choices, take actions, and respond to circumstances in ways that align with our values and goals.

Application

Try this four-step practice to develop greater skill in living fully in the present moment:

1. **Develop Present-Moment Awareness:** Throughout your day, practice regularly checking in with your current experience. Ask yourself: "What am I experiencing right now?" "What do

I see, hear, feel, taste, or smell at this moment?" "Where is my attention focused—on the past, future, or present?"

2. **Practice Mental Time Travel Recognition:** Notice when your mind drifts into unproductive past or future thinking. Common signs include feeling anxious (often future-focused), feeling depressed or regretful (often past-focused), or feeling disconnected from your current activity or the people around you. When you catch your mind time-traveling, gently acknowledge where it went and consciously redirect attention to something happening right now.

3. **Use Anchoring Techniques:** Develop specific practices that help you return to the present moment when you notice your mind has wandered. This might include taking three conscious breaths, noticing five things you can see in your current environment, feeling your feet on the ground, or focusing on physical sensations in your body.

4. **Find Present-Moment Gifts:** Actively look for aspects of your current experience that you can appreciate or engage with more fully. The goal is to develop a habit of recognizing the gifts available in each moment rather than constantly looking elsewhere for fulfillment or satisfaction.

Remember that developing present-moment living skills is a lifelong practice rather than a destination you reach. Your mind will continue to wander; that's normal and human. The skill lies in noticing when your attention has drifted and gently returning it to the current moment without self-criticism or frustration.

Also, understand that present-moment awareness doesn't mean never thinking about the past or future. Appropriate reflection and planning are valuable life skills. The key is being intentional about when you engage in past or future thinking rather than being unconsciously pulled away from the present by habitual mental patterns.

Most importantly, apply this practice to your relationships. When you're with family, friends, or colleagues, make a habit of giving them the gift of your full-present-moment attention. Put away distractions, listen actively, and focus on what's really happening in your shared experience right now instead of being mentally elsewhere.

Takeaway

Every moment you choose to be fully present rather than mentally elsewhere, you access the only time when life is actually happening and when you have real power to influence your experience and circumstances. You also give yourself and others the gift of genuine attention and authentic connection.

The most meaningful experiences in your life have likely occurred when you were fully present rather than thinking about something else. This isn't coincidental; presence is the doorway through which life's richest experiences become available to us.

The next time you notice your mind caught up in regrets about the past or anxieties about the future, remember Ted's wordplay and ask yourself: "What gifts are available to me in this present moment?" ""

After all, as Ted reminds us, the present moment truly is a gift—not because everything happening right now is pleasant or easy, but because the present is where life occurs, where choices are made, where relationships unfold, and where we could fully experience the remarkable fact of our own existence.

Living in the moment is indeed a gift. The question is whether you'll unwrap it.

Lesson #5:
The Power of Belief Beyond Symbols

The Example:

> Ted's Philosophy: *"Belief doesn't just happen because you hang something up on a wall. It comes from in here [heart], and up here [brain], down here [gut]."*
>
> --- Ted Lasso, Season 3, Episode 5: "Signs," after tearing down the "Believe" sign

Ted's emotional speech redefining "belief" comes from Season 3, Episode 5, titled "Signs." After the "Believe" sign is ripped down, Ted addresses the team with a heartfelt message about what belief truly means, shifting the focus from an external symbol to something internal and personal.

Ted's Speech Highlights (Season 3, Episode 5: "Signs")
Here are the highlights of Ted's speech to his team about the Believe sign.

"Belief doesn't just happen because you hang something up on a wall. All right? It comes from in here (heart). You know? And up here (brain). Down here (gut). The only problem is that we all have so much junk floating through us; a lot of times, we end up getting in our own way. You know, crap like envy, or fear, or shame. I don't want to mess around with that shit anymore. You know what I mean. Do you?

You know what I wanna mess around with? The belief that I matter... regardless of what I do or don't achieve. Or the belief that we all deserve to be loved, whether we've been hurt or maybe we've hurt somebody else. Or what about the belief of hope? Yeah? That's what I want to mess with.

Believing that things can get better. That I can get better. That we will get better.

Oh man. To believe in yourself. To believe in one another. Man, that's fundamental to being alive. And look, if you can do that, if each of you can truly do that, can't nobody rip that apart."

Context

Here is the context and setting for this speech:

- The "Believe" sign has been a symbol of team spirit and faith since Season 1, when Ted taped it above the locker room door.
- By Season 3, AFC Richmond is struggling badly, and the "Believe" mantra feels hollow to the players.
- Tensions are rising: Zava (the star player) is unreliable, Rebecca is losing confidence in Ted, and the team's cohesion is falling apart.
- In frustration, Ted tears down the "Believe" sign that has hung over the locker room since his arrival.
- The players are stunned. It feels like the symbol of their hope is being destroyed.
- Ted's speech explains that belief can't come from a poster or an external slogan. Instead, it must be internal—rooted in the heart (passion), the brain (conviction), and the gut (courage/instinct).

Meaning and Impact

Ted redefines belief as something more profound and more personal than just a sign on the wall. It is about hope, self-worth, resilience, and compassion within oneself and the team. This moment marks a turning point, reminding the team (and viewers) that true belief is internal and unwavering, regardless of setbacks. Ted's speech is recognized as one of the most powerful and inspirational moments in the series, guiding his players to find belief within themselves and one another, not just in external symbols.

The famous "Believe" sign symbolizes one of the most powerful icons in Ted Lasso, but its true importance isn't in the physical sign itself. Instead, it highlights Ted's key lesson that genuine belief must come from within. The handwritten yellow sign with "BELIEVE" in all caps serves as a focal point to explore what real faith, hope, and confidence truly mean.

The BELIEVE Sign Evolution

It's helpful to review the evolution of the Believe sign from its first introduction in the first episode, through its destruction and return.

The Sign's First Appearance and Initial Reception

The "Believe" sign makes its debut in the very first episode, Season 1, Episode 1: "Pilot," as one of Ted's first acts when he arrives at AFC Richmond. Ted hangs the simple, handwritten sign above the door to the coaches' office in the locker room, though it goes up slightly crooked. Keeley Jones helps him adjust it, creating a bonding moment between them and the beginning of their friendship.

The initial reaction from players is mixed, ranging from skepticism to outright dismissal. Early in the series, it became clear that Ted's can-do attitude wasn't enough to turn the team around on its own, and his Believe sign was looked upon with a fair amount of skepticism. The players see it as typical American optimism—naive, simplistic, and potentially embarrassing in the hardened world of English Premier League football.

Evolution of the Sign's Meaning

As Season 1 progresses, the sign gradually transforms from an object of ridicule into a source of genuine inspiration. While it seemed silly at first, it soon became a rallying point for not only the players but also the team's coaching staff and even Ted himself, who often struggled with his own problems off the field.

The turning point happens during critical matches when players start engaging with the sign in meaningful ways. When the team's morale is low after losing at halftime, Isaac touches the "BELIEVE" sign on the wall, followed by the rest of the team, while the coaches, including Roy Kent (minus Nate) and Will Kitman, watch proudly. This moment shows that the sign has become more than just decoration. It has become a ritual, a source of connection and shared purpose.

Nate's Betrayal and the Sign's Destruction

The most dramatic moment in the sign's history happens at the end of Season 2, when Nathan Shelley tears it in half in a heartbreaking act of betrayal. After their victory against Man City, Nate heads to the locker room, takes down the poster, rips it in half, and drops it on Ted's desk. During the shocking Season 2 finale, Nate tears the Believe sign in half, which reveals as much about him as it does about Ted and his personal philosophy. Ultimately, Nate feels insecure about his place in the locker room, and faith alone isn't enough for him to get through.

Ted's response to this betrayal reveals his character and wisdom. Ted doesn't tell the team and the coaches that Nate ripped the sign poster in half, only discreetly taped back the poster and hang it on the wall above the office again. He protects both Nate's reputation and the team's morale by quietly repairing the damage without making it a dramatic confrontation.

The Sign's Use as Motivation and Weapon

In Season 3, the destroyed sign becomes both a source of motivation and a weapon. After a rough first half [against West Ham], Coach Beard and Roy show Richmond some footage found by Trent Crimm of Nate ripping up the "Believe" sign from the end of season two when AFC Richmond was promoted back to the English Premier League. The team becomes quite angry and walks back onto the pitch staring angrily at Nate. This results in them becoming angry and anarchic as the players start to play dirty and chaotic in the match.

This moment reveals how symbols can be weaponized and how external motivation based on anger or revenge ultimately proves destructive rather than constructive.

Ted's Ultimate Teaching: Beyond the Symbol

The culmination of the sign's journey comes in Season 3, Episode 5: "Signs," when Ted delivers perhaps his most profound teaching about the nature of belief. When half the "Believe" sign falls from the wall, he tears up the rest of it, saying it's "just a sign" and that their belief in themselves and each other cannot be ripped apart.

Ted's complete speech provides the philosophical foundation: "Belief doesn't just happen because you hang something up on a wall. All right? It comes from in here (heart). You know? And up here (brain). Down here (gut). Only problem is we all got so much junk floating through us, a lot of times we end up getting in our own way. You know, crap like envy, or fear, shame. I don't want to mess around with that shit anymore. You know what I mean. Do you?... You know what I wanna mess around with? The belief that I matter... regardless of what I do or don't achieve. Or the belief that we all deserve to be loved, whether we've been hurt or maybe we've hurt somebody else. Or what about the belief of hope?"

The Players' Secret and Final Redemption

The story of the Believe sign reaches its most touching conclusion in the series finale. Unbeknownst to Ted, the team players keep the pieces of the ripped Believe poster for themselves. All the members put each piece within them for good luck. As Ted encourages the team when they are playing against West Ham, Sam Obisanya shows his coaches that they still have the pieces. The players put together the pieces of the poster into whole again, while Nate looks in awe, Trent Crimm looks mesmerized, and Ted looks proud.

Nate uses the Japanese art of kintsugi to repair Ted's "Believe" sign, painting over the tears with gold and rehanging it in the Greyhounds' locker room. This beautiful gesture shows that belief, like the sign itself, can be broken and repaired, often emerging stronger and more beautiful than before.

Explanation

The journey of the "Believe" sign throughout Ted Lasso represents a profound exploration of the difference between superficial symbols and authentic faith. The sign serves as a vehicle for examining how beliefs develop, how they can be manipulated, and ultimately where genuine conviction must originate to have lasting power and meaning.

Initially, the sign functions as what psychologists call an "external locus of control." The players and even some viewers see it as something outside themselves that might magically influence outcomes. This represents a common but ultimately limited understanding of belief, where faith is treated as a superstition or lucky charm rather than an internal state of confidence and commitment.

The evolution of players' relationship with the sign mirrors the psychological journey from external to internal motivation. Research in motivation theory shows that external motivators (like symbols, rewards, or threats) can provide short-term behavior change but rarely create lasting transformation. Internal motivation—driven by personal values, intrinsic satisfaction, and authentic conviction—proves far more sustainable and powerful.

Nate's destruction of the sign represents more than vandalism; it's a rejection of the entire belief system the sign symbolizes. His action reveals his fundamental misunderstanding of what Ted was trying to teach. Nate believed that destroying the physical symbol would destroy the team's faith, demonstrating that he never internalized the deeper lesson about where true belief originates.

Ted's response to the sign's destruction, quietly repairing it without drama or blame, shows mature leadership and an authentic understanding of what the sign represents. He protects both Nate (by not exposing him) and the team (by not letting the destruction become a crisis), because he understands that the real power was never in the physical sign but in what it helped people discover within themselves.

The weaponization of the sign's destruction in Season 3 provides a cautionary lesson about how symbols can be manipulated to create negative motivation. When Coach Beard and Roy show the team footage of Nate tearing the sign, it generates anger and revenge-seeking behavior that ultimately proves destructive. This demonstrates that even positive symbols can be corrupted when used to fuel negative emotions rather than constructive growth.

Ted's ultimate teaching moment, when he tears down the remaining sign and explains that belief comes from within, represents the culmination of the entire series' exploration of faith and confidence. He's essentially teaching the team (and viewers) to graduate from symbol-dependent faith to self-generated belief. This represents psychological and spiritual maturity: the ability to maintain conviction and hope even when external symbols or circumstances change.

The players' secret preservation of the sign's pieces shows how powerful symbols can be when properly internalized. They kept the pieces not as superstitious talismans but as reminders of the internal qualities they had developed. The final reconstruction of the sign represents not a return to symbol-dependence but a celebration of the internal growth that the symbol helped facilitate.

Application

Try this expanded four-step practice to develop authentic belief beyond external symbols:

1. **Examine Your Symbol Dependencies:** Identify the external symbols, rituals, or objects you rely on for confidence, motivation, or belief in yourself and your goals. This might include lucky charms, specific clothing, environmental conditions, or the approval of others.

2. **Identify Your Core Beliefs:** Like Ted's speech about believing "that I matter regardless of what I do or don't achieve," identify the fundamental beliefs that support your confidence and resilience. What do you believe about your inherent worth? About your capacity to grow and learn? About your ability to handle challenges? About the possibility of a positive change in your life?

3. **Practice Internal Belief Building:** Develop specific practices that strengthen your internal sources of conviction and confidence. This might include daily affirmations that reflect

your core values, regular reflection on your growth and progress, meditation or mindfulness practices that connect you with your inner wisdom, or exercises that help you recognize your inherent capabilities and worth. The key is building habits that reinforce internal sources of strength rather than relying solely on external validation or symbols.

4. **Test and Strengthen Your Belief System:** Deliberately put yourself in situations where you must rely on internal conviction rather than external support. This might mean pursuing goals without others' immediate approval, maintaining confidence during setbacks or criticism, or persisting in important work even when external rewards aren't immediately visible. Use these experiences to identify where your belief system is strong and where it needs further development.

Remember that symbols and external supports aren't inherently bad. They can serve valuable functions in reminding us of our values and connecting us with others who share our beliefs. The key is ensuring that these external elements support rather than replace internal conviction and self-generated faith.

Also understand that developing internal belief is an ongoing process, not a destination you reach once and maintain effortlessly. Like the players who kept pieces of the sign as personal reminders, you can use external symbols as tools for internal development rather than crutches for external dependence.

Most importantly, recognize that your ability to believe in yourself, your goals, and the possibility of positive change doesn't depend on perfect circumstances, universal approval, or magical symbols. Like Ted teaches, authentic belief comes from your heart, mind, and gut—internal resources that no one can take away from you and that grow stronger with use and practice.

Takeaway

Every time you choose to draw strength from internal conviction rather than external symbols, you build the kind of resilient, sustainable belief that can weather any storm and survive any betrayal. You also model for others what authentic faith looks like and create the possibility for deeper, more meaningful confidence that doesn't depend on circumstances beyond your control.

The most powerful belief isn't the kind that depends on favorable conditions, supportive symbols, or other people's approval. It's the kind that emerges from a deep understanding of your own worth, capabilities, and potential for growth. This internal foundation provides stability and strength that no external force can destroy or diminish.

The next time you notice yourself becoming overly dependent on external symbols or validation for your confidence, remember Ted's wisdom and ask yourself: "What would I believe about myself and my possibilities if I had to rely solely on my internal resources?" "How can I strengthen the beliefs that come from my heart, mind, and gut?" "What would change if my faith were truly internal rather than dependent on external symbols?"

After all, as the entire journey of the "Believe" sign demonstrates, symbols can be torn down, stolen, or destroyed, but authentic belief. It's the kind that comes from within and can't be ripped apart. That's not just good coaching. It's the foundation for a life built on unshakeable internal strength and genuine self-confidence.

Belief doesn't just happen because you hang something up on a wall. It happens when you discover the unbreakable source of strength that was inside you all along.

Lesson #6:
Create Your Own Luck

The Example:

Ted's quote: *"The harder you work, the luckier you get."*

--- Ted Lasso, Season 1, Episode 1: "Pilot"

This quote appears early in Ted's journey at AFC Richmond, delivered with his characteristic blend of folksy wisdom and genuine insight. The setting is significant: Ted is still finding his footing in an entirely foreign environment, facing skepticism from players, media, and fans who doubt his ability to succeed in English football. Yet rather than being discouraged by the enormity of the challenge ahead, Ted offers this perspective on how success really works.

Context

Here are the background, setting, and context for Ted Lasso's quote:

- Ted Lasso, the American football coach, arrives in England as the new manager of the struggling soccer team AFC Richmond.
- In the pilot episode, Ted faces skepticism and ridicule from players, staff, media, and fans who doubt his qualifications and believe he's destined to fail.
- Ted's attitude is relentlessly optimistic; he brings American-style hope and work ethic to a club and culture where cynicism has taken root.

- Ted offers this quote early in the series to the team, media, and staff as part of his overall motivational philosophy.
- He uses the phrase to emphasize the importance of determination, effort, and perseverance, independent of whether initial results are positive or negative.
- The statement inspires his players and establishes Ted's leadership style: hard work, positive thinking, and faith in self and team will create opportunities even if others dismiss the club's prospects.
- The quote is widely attributed to golfer Gary Player, who famously said, "The harder you work, the luckier you get."

It encapsulates a belief that preparation and persistent effort often create 'luck' and Ted Lasso adapts Gary Player's legendary maxim as a central pillar of his coaching approach, transforming AFC Richmond's culture from one of resignation to one of hope and possibility, beginning in the very first episode.

The quote occurs during one of Ted's early interactions as he gets to know his new environment and establishes his coaching philosophy. It's particularly meaningful because Ted himself is about to embark on what many would consider an impossible task, coaching a sport he knows little about, in a country where he's an outsider, with a team that's been set up to fail. By sharing this belief about the relationship between effort and opportunity, Ted is essentially laying out his roadmap for turning an unlikely situation into a success story.

The Context of an Impossible Challenge

When Ted arrives at AFC Richmond, almost everything is stacked against him. He has no experience coaching soccer, he's unfamiliar with English football culture, the media is openly hostile, the players are skeptical, and unbeknownst to him, his own boss, Rebecca, has hired him specifically hoping he'll fail. By conventional measures, Ted should have almost no chance of success.

Yet Ted approaches this challenge with the fundamental belief that consistent effort and preparation can create opportunities that others might attribute to luck. This isn't naive optimism—it's a strategic mindset that recognizes how preparation intersects with opportunity to create what appears to be fortunate outcomes.

Throughout the pilot episode, we see Ted embodying this philosophy in practical ways. He studies the team, learns players' names, observes their dynamics, and begins building relationships. While others might see his eventual successes as surprising or lucky, Ted is systematically creating the conditions that will make positive outcomes more likely.

The Mechanics of "Making" Luck

Ted's quote reflects a sophisticated understanding of how perceived luck actually works. What most people call luck is often the result of preparation meeting opportunity, persistence creating breakthrough moments, and consistent effort eventually yielding unexpected positive results.

This becomes evident throughout Ted's tenure at Richmond. His success in connecting with players like Sam Obisanya, Roy Kent, and eventually even Jamie Tartt doesn't happen by accident—it's the result of Ted's consistent efforts to understand, support, and believe in each individual. When these relationships pay off in crucial moments, it might appear lucky, but it's actually the predictable result of Ted's investment in people.

Similarly, Ted's tactical innovations and team-building strategies often produce results that seem surprisingly good given his lack of traditional soccer experience. But these aren't random lucky breaks—they're the outcome of Ted's willingness to study, experiment, collaborate with Coach Beard and others, and adapt his American football knowledge to a different sport.

The Compound Effect of Consistent Effort

Throughout Season 1, we see how Ted's daily habits and consistent approaches accumulate into larger successes. His practice of bringing biscuits to Rebecca, his genuine interest in learning players' names and backgrounds, his willingness to admit what he doesn't know while working hard to learn—these small, consistent efforts create a compound effect that transforms relationships and outcomes.

The "harder you work, the luckier you get" philosophy is particularly evident in Ted's approach to problem-solving. When faced with challenges he doesn't understand, instead of hoping for lucky breaks, Ted increases his effort: he asks more questions, seeks more input, tries new approaches, and persists through setbacks. This active approach to difficulty creates more opportunities for positive outcomes than passive hoping ever could.

Examples Throughout the Series

This philosophy plays out repeatedly across all three seasons of the show. When Richmond faces relegation at the end of Season 1, Ted's preparation and relationship-building pay off in unexpected ways. The players' willingness to try his unconventional "Lasso Special" play comes not from luck but from the trust he's built through consistent effort and genuine care.

In Season 2, when Ted faces personal challenges, including panic attacks and marital problems, his continued commitment to hard work, both professionally and in seeking help for his mental health, creates opportunities for growth and healing that might appear fortunate but are actually the result of his willingness to do difficult work on himself.

Season 3 shows the ultimate fruition of Ted's philosophy as many of his long-term investments in people and relationships yield significant positive results. Characters like Jamie Tartt's redemption, Roy Kent's coaching development, and Rebecca's personal growth all represent "lucky" outcomes that are actually the predictable results of Ted's consistent faith, effort, and support over time.

The Psychology of Effort and Opportunity

Ted's quote reflects important psychological principles about how mindset affects outcomes. People who believe that effort creates opportunity (what psychologists call an "internal locus of control") are more likely to persist through difficulties, notice potential solutions, and take actions that increase their chances of success.

This contrasts with people who attribute outcomes primarily to external factors or random chance. Those with an external locus of control are more likely to give up when faced with obstacles, miss opportunities that require effort to recognize, and remain passive when action could improve their situation.

Ted consistently demonstrates the internal locus of control mindset. He doesn't wait for lucky breaks or blame external circumstances when things go wrong. Instead, he asks what he can do, how he can improve, and where he can invest more effort to create better outcomes.

Explanation

The relationship between effort and luck is one of the most misunderstood dynamics in human achievement and well-being. Most people think of luck as completely random—good things that happen to us without any connection to our actions or preparation. This perspective, while partially accurate, misses the crucial ways that our choices, habits, and efforts influence what appears to be fortunate or unfortunate outcomes.

Ted's philosophy recognizes that while we cannot control all external circumstances, we have far more influence over our "luck" than most people realize. What we often call luck is actually the intersection of preparation and opportunity, persistence and breakthrough, or consistent effort and eventual positive results.

This concept has deep roots in achievement psychology and performance research. Studies consistently show that people who achieve high levels of success in any field typically combine natural ability with extraordinary amounts of deliberate practice and preparation. When these highly prepared individuals encounter opportunities, they're able to capitalize on them in ways that appear lucky to outside observers but are actually predictable outcomes of their preparation.

The "harder you work, the luckier you get" mindset also creates a positive feedback loop. When you believe that effort increases the probability of positive outcomes, you're more likely to maintain high levels of effort even when immediate results aren't visible. This persistence often leads to breakthroughs that seem sudden to others but represent the culmination of sustained work.

Additionally, hard work often increases your visibility and reputation, which creates more opportunities for "lucky" breaks. When you're known as someone who consistently delivers high-quality effort, people are more likely to think of you when opportunities arise, recommend you for positions, or seek your collaboration on interesting projects.

The psychology behind this philosophy also involves attention and recognition. People who work hard in pursuit of goals become more attuned to opportunities related to those goals. They notice possibilities that others miss, recognize patterns that lead to solutions, and develop the expertise necessary to act quickly when chances present themselves.

However, it's important to acknowledge that this philosophy must be balanced with recognition of genuine systemic barriers and random circumstances that affect outcomes regardless of effort. Not all inequality or difficulty can be overcome through hard work alone, and the "harder you work, the luckier you get" mindset can become problematic if it's used to blame people for circumstances beyond their control.

The healthiest application of Ted's philosophy focuses on what you can influence while acknowledging what you cannot. It emphasizes maximizing your preparation and effort within your sphere of control while remaining realistic about external factors that may help or hinder your progress.

Application

Try this four-step practice to start creating your own luck through strategic effort:

1. **Identify Your Opportunity Areas:** Look at areas of your life where you hope for better outcomes and honestly assess how much effort you're currently investing. Ask yourself: "Where am I waiting for lucky breaks instead of working to create opportunities?" "

2. **Increase Your Preparation Systematically:** Choose one area where you want better "luck" and commit to significantly

increasing your preparation and effort. The key is consistent, deliberate effort rather than sporadic, intense bursts.

3. **Develop Opportunity Recognition Skills:** Train yourself to notice and act on possibilities that others might miss. This involves staying alert to your environment, asking questions that reveal hidden opportunities, and maintaining a mindset that looks for solutions rather than dwelling on problems.

4. **Build Resilience for Long-Term Effort:** Recognize that the "harder you work, the luckier you get" philosophy requires sustained effort over time, not just short-term intensity.

Remember that creating your own luck is a long-term strategy, not a quick fix. The most significant "lucky" breakthroughs often come after months or years of preparation that seemed to produce little immediate benefit. Trust the process and maintain effort even when progress feels slow.

Also, understand that increasing your effort doesn't guarantee specific outcomes. It increases the probability of positive outcomes while helping you develop resilience and skills that serve you regardless of particular results. Sometimes your hard work pays off in ways you didn't expect or in areas you weren't specifically targeting.

Most importantly, apply this philosophy with wisdom and compassion, both for yourself and others. While effort dramatically influences outcomes, it doesn't eliminate all randomness or overcome all systemic barriers. Use Ted's philosophy to maximize your agency and preparation while maintaining realistic expectations about what you can and cannot control.

Takeaway

Every time you choose to increase your effort, preparation, and persistence rather than waiting for external circumstances to change, you shift the odds in your favor and create more opportunities for positive outcomes. You also develop the skills, relationships, and resilience that make you better prepared to capitalize on opportunities when they arise. The most successful people aren't necessarily those who experience the most random good fortune. They're those who have learned to create conditions that make positive outcomes more likely. They understand that what appears to be luck is often the predictable result of consistent effort, careful preparation, and persistent pursuit of their goals.

The next time you find yourself hoping for a lucky break or wishing circumstances were different, remember Ted's wisdom and ask yourself: "What can I do to increase the probability of the outcome I want?" "How can I better prepare for opportunities that might arise?" "What consistent efforts could I make that would compound into significant advantages over time?"

After all, as Ted demonstrates throughout his journey at AFC Richmond, the most reliable way to improve your luck is to outwork it. When you combine genuine effort with patience and persistence, you create a powerful force that can overcome many obstacles and generate opportunities that others might attribute to fortune. Still, you'll know the result from your commitment to doing the work.

The harder you work, the luckier you get. It's not magic; it's mathematics. And it's available to anyone willing to do the work.

Lesson #7:
Authentic Apologies and Acceptance

The Example:

Rebecca's specific apology to Ted in Season 1, Episode 9 ("All Apologies") is:

"Ted, I lied to you. I hired you because I wanted this team to lose. I wanted you to fail, and I sabotaged you every chance I got. It was me who hired that photographer to take the photo of you and Keeley. I set up the interview with Trent Crimm, hoping that he would humiliate you. And I instigated the transfer of Jamie Tartt, even though you'd asked me not to. This club is all that Rupert has ever cared about, and I wanted to destroy it. To cause him as much pain and suffering as he has caused me. And I didn't care who I used or who I hurt. All you good people just trying to make a difference. Ted, I'm so sorry. If you want to quit or call the press, I'll completely understand."

Ted's response is: *"I forgive you."*

When Rebecca asks, *"You... What? Why?"*

Ted replies: *"Divorce is hard. It doesn't matter if you're the one leaving or if... you're the one who got left. It makes folks do crazy things."*

This exchange showcases Rebecca's sincere remorse and Ted's profound empathy and capacity for forgiveness, solidifying one of the show's most poignant moments of redemption and grace.

Rebecca's apology to Ted in episode 9 ("All Apologies") occurs after a season-long arc where Rebecca, the owner of AFC

Richmond, has been secretly working to undermine Ted as part of her revenge against her ex-husband, Rupert. Ted's persistent kindness and optimism gradually wear down Rebecca's defenses, and Rebecca faces mounting pressure from Keeley to own up to her behaviors. After Rupert delivers the emotionally devastating news that he and his new wife are expecting a child, a dream he had always denied Rebecca, she is pushed over the edge emotionally, prompting her to finally confess her sabotage to Ted.

Context for the Apology
- Rebecca originally hired Ted with the intention that his lack of soccer experience would ruin the team and thus hurt Rupert, her ex-husband, who loved the club.
- Throughout the season, Rebecca orchestrates various schemes, including leaking personal information about players and manufacturing negative press, all aimed at destabilizing the club.
- Keeley persistently encourages Rebecca to be honest, highlighting the importance of accountability and vulnerability, reinforcing the season's themes of growth and forgiveness.
- In episode 9, the pressure reaches a peak after Rebecca receives news from Rupert that he is expecting a child with his new wife. The cruelty of this revelation is magnified by the fact that Rupert once claimed not to want children during his marriage to Rebecca.
- Feeling broken and realizing her attempts to hurt Rupert have yielded nothing but further pain for herself and others, Rebecca decides to come clean.
- She approaches Ted in his office and tearfully confesses to all her sabotage. Ted listens and responds with immediate forgiveness, drawing on his own experiences with divorce and recognizing her pain.
- Ted's forgiveness is central to the show's message of empathy and compassion. He says, "If you care about someone and you've got a little love in your heart, there ain't nothing you can't get through together," extending understanding to Rebecca in her lowest moment.

- The scene marks a major turning point for Rebecca, allowing her to start making amends with other characters and paving the way for her emotional growth throughout the rest of the series.
- Critics have praised the scene as emotionally powerful, both for its vulnerability and the way it exemplifies the possibility for redemption through honest apology and forgiveness.

Rebecca's apology is a culmination of her internal struggle with guilt and pain; Ted's response sets the thematic tone for accountability and healing in the series.

While Ted Lasso frequently models the art of authentic apologies throughout the series, the principle of taking full responsibility for our mistakes is most powerfully illustrated not through Ted's own words but through how his example inspires others to make genuine amends.

This episode serves as an example of what authentic accountability looks like, contrasting genuine apologies with empty ones, and demonstrating how real remorse can transform relationships and heal communities.

**Rebecca's Transformation:
From Manipulation to Accountability**

Throughout the first season, Rebecca has been systematically sabotaging AFC Richmond as part of her revenge plot against her ex-husband Rupert. She hired Ted, hoping he would fail spectacularly, arranged for paparazzi to create scandals, set up hostile interviews, and manipulated player transfers. All while presenting herself as supportive and professional to Ted's face.

The breaking point comes when Keeley confronts Rebecca with evidence of her scheme, particularly the hired photographer incident. In a crucial conversation, Keeley tells Rebecca that she must come clean immediately or she will go to Ted herself. This forces Rebecca to face a moment of truth: she can continue hiding behind her justifications or finally take responsibility for the harm she's caused. When Rebecca finally enters Ted's office to confess, her apology becomes one of the most emotionally powerful scenes in the series.

The Anatomy of an Authentic Apology

Rebecca's confession demonstrates every element of what makes an apology genuine and transformative:

- **Complete Ownership**: She doesn't minimize, justify, or make excuses. She states clearly what she did and takes full responsibility.
- **Specific Acknowledgment:** Rather than offering a vague "I'm sorry if I hurt you," she details exactly what actions she took and how they were intended to cause harm.
- **Recognition of Impact:** She acknowledges that her actions affected not just Ted but "all you good people just trying to make a difference."
- **Expression of Genuine Remorse:** Her apology stems from a place of authentic regret, not just because she was caught, but because she genuinely acknowledges the wrongfulness of her actions.
- **No Conditions or Expectations:** She doesn't ask for forgiveness or try to control Ted's response. She accepts that he might quit or expose her publicly.

Ted's Response:
Modeling Grace and Understanding

What makes this scene even more powerful is Ted's response. Rather than responding with anger or condemnation, Ted demonstrates extraordinary grace and understanding. As Rebecca later tells Higgins: "You know what the little shit did? He forgave me." Higgins responds: "Fucking arsehole." Rebecca: "I know!" This humorous exchange reveals how Ted's immediate forgiveness was both unexpected and transformative.

Ted's response teaches us that receiving an authentic apology with grace can be just as powerful as offering one. He understands that Rebecca's actions came from her own pain and trauma from her divorce, and he chooses compassion over condemnation.

The Ripple Effect of Authentic Accountability

Rebecca's authentic apology to Ted creates a ripple effect of accountability throughout the episode. After confessing to Ted, Rebecca continues her apology tour by visiting Higgins. Rebecca apologizes to him for treating him so poorly during her childish scheming and promises she's on her way back to her old self, which Higgins recognizes.

This demonstrates another crucial aspect of authentic apologies: they often reveal a pattern of harm that requires multiple acts of accountability. Rebecca doesn't stop with Ted. She recognizes that her behavior has affected others and takes responsibility across the board.

Contrasting Authentic and Empty Apologies

The series also shows us what empty apologies look like. In Season 1, Episode 4 ("For the Children"), when Jamie brings a second date to the charity auction without telling Keeley, he later approaches her and says he's sorry. But when Keeley asks what he's sorry for, he doesn't have an answer, at which point Keeley dumps him. This scene perfectly illustrates the difference between saying "I'm sorry" and actually understanding what you're apologizing for.

The Broader Pattern of Accountability

Throughout the series, Ted consistently models how to take responsibility for mistakes. As one observer notes: "I don't think it's a coincidence that I've observed a sincere apology in almost every episode. In the show, we see a player apologize to his team for consistently disrespecting them, a coach apologizes to a player for not taking into consideration global imperialism (!), a person apologizes to a romantic partner for not showing trust, a journalist apologizes to a public figure for defaming him, and a parent apologize to a child for not being present."

Explanation

The art of authentic apology is one of the most undervalued and misunderstood skills in human relationships. In our culture, we're often taught that apologizing is a sign of weakness, that admitting mistakes makes us vulnerable to attack, or that saying "I'm sorry" is sufficient to repair any damage we've caused. These misconceptions prevent us from accessing one of the most powerful tools available for healing relationships, building trust, and creating the conditions for genuine growth and connection.

The fundamental difference between an authentic apology and an empty one lies in the motivation behind it. Empty apologies are often strategic, designed to end an uncomfortable conversation, avoid consequences, or manipulate the other person into "getting over it" quickly. Authentic apologies, by contrast, emerge from genuine recognition of harm caused and a sincere desire to repair the damage and prevent future harm.

An authentic apology requires several key elements that distinguish it from its hollow counterparts. First, it demands complete ownership of the behavior without excuses, justifications, or attempts to shift blame. When Rebecca confesses to Ted, she doesn't say, "I divorce hurt me, so I sabotaged you." Instead, she takes full responsibility for her choices and actions, regardless of what prompted them.

Second, authentic apologies are specific rather than vague. Saying "I'm sorry if I hurt you" or "I'm sorry you feel that way" actually shifts responsibility to the injured party and minimizes the impact of the harm. Genuine apologies name the specific actions taken and acknowledge their impact: "I did this specific thing, and it caused this specific harm."

Third, real apologies express genuine remorse—not just regret at being caught or facing consequences, but authentic sorrow for the pain caused. This remorse must be accompanied by a clear understanding of why the behavior was wrong, not just because it had negative consequences, but because it violated important principles or values.

Fourth, authentic apologies don't come with conditions, timelines, or expectations. They don't include phrases like "I've apologized, so you need to get over it" or "How long are you going to stay mad about this?" The person offering the apology must be prepared to accept that forgiveness may not come immediately, or at all, and that earning back trust will likely require consistent changed behavior over time.

Perhaps most importantly, authentic apologies must be followed by changed behavior. As the saying goes, "An apology without changed behavior is just manipulation." The most eloquent confession in the world means nothing if the harmful behavior continues. Real accountability requires not just acknowledging past mistakes but taking concrete steps to ensure they don't happen again.

The psychological benefits of offering authentic apologies are profound. When we take full responsibility for our mistakes, we free ourselves from the exhausting work of maintaining defensive stories and justifications. We stop using mental energy to protect our ego and can redirect that energy toward learning, growing, and building better relationships. Authentic accountability also strengthens rather than weakens our character and reputation. While it might seem counterintuitive, people generally respect and trust those who can acknowledge their mistakes more than those who never admit to being wrong. The latter seems either dishonest or lacking in self-awareness, while the former demonstrates integrity, humility, and a commitment to growth.

For the person receiving an authentic apology, the experience can be equally transformative. Being truly seen and acknowledged in your pain, having the harm validated rather than minimized, and witnessing genuine remorse can begin the healing process in ways that nothing else can. It doesn't erase the harm, but it creates the possibility for repair and renewed trust.

Application

Try this four-step practice to help you master the art of authentic apology:

1. **Develop Self-Awareness and Take Inventory:** Regularly examine your behavior and its impact on others, even when no one is complaining or confronting you. You can cause harm even when your intentions were good, and impact matters regardless of intent. Consider asking trusted friends or

family members for honest feedback about areas where you might need to improve.

2. **Craft Specific, Complete Apologies:** When you recognize you've caused harm, prepare to take full responsibility without conditions or justifications. Use this structure: "I [specific action you took]. I understand this caused [specific impact or harm]. I was wrong because [why the behavior violated important values or principles]. I am genuinely sorry, and I want to [specific actions you'll take to repair and prevent future harm]." Avoid phrases like "I'm sorry if you were hurt," "I'm sorry, but..." or "I didn't mean to..." Focus on what you did and its impact, not on your intentions or circumstances.

3. **Follow Through with Changed Behavior:** Understand that an apology is just the beginning of accountability, not the end. Identify the underlying patterns, triggers, or systems that contributed to the harmful behavior and address them directly: forgiveness or a return to the previous relationship dynamic.

4. **Create a Culture of Accountability:** In your family, workplace, or community, model and encourage authentic accountability from everyone. This means receiving others' apologies with grace when they're genuine, having honest conversations about harm and impact.

Remember that learning to apologize authentically is itself a skill that improves with practice. Your first attempts might feel awkward or incomplete, and that's normal. The important thing is to start developing the habits of self-reflection, ownership, and genuine care for others that make authentic accountability possible. Also, understand that not everyone will respond to authentic apologies the way Ted responds to Rebecca.

Most importantly, recognize that your willingness to be genuinely accountable sets an example that ripples outward, creating permission for others to do the same. When people see you taking real responsibility for your mistakes, they're more likely to examine their own behavior and take steps to repair harm they may have caused.

Takeaway

Every time you choose to offer an authentic apology instead of making excuses, minimizing harm, or deflecting responsibility, you strengthen the fabric of trust that holds relationships and communities together. You also demonstrate that it's possible to make mistakes and still be a person of integrity—in fact, how we handle our mistakes is often the truest test of our character.

The most powerful apologies don't just repair past harm. They prevent future harm by creating deeper understanding, stronger relationships, and better systems for navigating conflict and difficulty. When you can look someone in the eye and say, "I was wrong, I caused harm, I understand the impact, and I'm committed to doing better," you create the possibility for a relationship and community that can withstand the inevitable imperfections of human interaction. The next time you realize you've made a mistake or caused harm, remember Rebecca's courage in facing Ted with the full truth, and Ted's grace in receiving that truth with understanding. Ask yourself: "What would it look like to take complete responsibility without justification or excuse?" "How can I acknowledge the specific harm I've caused?" "What concrete steps can I take to repair the damage and prevent similar harm in the future?"

After all, as Ted Lasso consistently demonstrates, the goal isn't to be perfect; it's to be accountable. And in a world where so many people are quick to blame others and slow to examine themselves, your willingness to say "I was wrong, I'm sorry, and here's how I'm going to do better" becomes a gift not just to those you've harmed, but to everyone who witnesses what authentic accountability looks like.

That's not just good relationship skills; it's good humanity.

Lesson #8:
Let Go and Move Forward

The Example:

> Ted's quote: "*You know what the happiest animal on Earth is? It's a goldfish. Got a 10-second memory. Be a goldfish, Sam.*"
>
> --- Ted Lasso to Sam Obisanya, Season 1, Episode 2: "Biscuits"

This memorable piece of advice comes during one of Ted's early interactions with Sam Obisanya, a young Nigerian defender who's struggling with a mistake he made during a match. Sam is clearly dwelling on his error, replaying it in his mind and allowing it to affect his confidence and future performance. Rather than offering a complex psychological analysis or demanding that Sam "get over it," Ted delivers one of his most famous metaphors about resilience and mental recovery.

Context
- Ted Lasso delivers this advice as a metaphor, encouraging players to forget mistakes or failures quickly and move forward with optimism and focus.
- The goldfish analogy is used repeatedly in the series, establishing Ted's unconventional coaching style focused on positivity, resilience, and emotional well-being rather than just tactical expertise.
- The scene takes place early in the show when Sam feels discouraged after a poor performance, and Ted uses the

"goldfish" wisdom to help boost his spirits and keep him from dwelling on errors.
- This philosophy of "be a goldfish" becomes an important ethos for the whole team, spreading Ted's message of short-term memory for mistakes and long-term commitment to personal growth.
- Ted's approach is contrasted with traditional tough coaching, effectively fostering an environment of emotional safety, positivity, and teambuilding.
- The quote exemplifies Ted's leadership style and is often cited as a signature moment for the series, endearing fans to his empathetic, uplifting approach

The goldfish analogy, while scientifically inaccurate (goldfish actually have much longer memories than 10 seconds), captures a profound truth about psychological well-being and performance: the ability to let go of past mistakes and approach each new moment with a fresh perspective is essential for happiness, growth, and success.

Sam's Struggle

In this early episode, Sam represents many of the players who are still adjusting to Ted's unconventional coaching style and philosophy. Coming from a different football culture and background, Sam initially struggles to understand how Ted's approach to mistakes and setbacks differs from more traditional, punitive coaching methods he may have experienced before.

When Sam makes an error during the match, his natural response is to carry that mistake forward, allowing it to compound into ongoing anxiety and self-doubt. This is a common pattern for athletes and indeed for most people. We tend to hold onto negative experiences, replaying them and allowing them to influence our confidence and decision-making going forward. Ted recognizes this pattern immediately and intervenes with his goldfish metaphor before Sam's mistake can snowball into a larger psychological barrier. The timing is crucial: Ted doesn't wait for Sam to "work through" his feelings or spend extensive time processing the error. Instead, he offers an immediate framework for moving forward.

The Deeper Wisdom of the Goldfish Philosophy

While the goldfish memory metaphor is scientifically imprecise, it represents several important psychological principles that are backed by research. First, it embodies the concept of "psychological flexibility"—the ability to adapt our thinking and behavior to changing circumstances rather than getting stuck in rigid patterns of rumination and self-criticism.

Second, the goldfish philosophy aligns with mindfulness principles about living in the present moment rather than being trapped by past experiences or future anxieties. When Ted tells Sam to "be a goldfish," he's essentially encouraging a form of present-moment awareness that allows for peak performance and emotional well-being.

Third, this approach recognizes that dwelling on mistakes often creates more problems than the original error did. In sports psychology, this is known as the "mistake spiral"—where one error leads to overthinking, which leads to tension, which leads to more mistakes, creating a downward cycle that can destroy confidence and performance.

Applications Throughout the Series

The goldfish philosophy becomes a recurring theme that Ted applies not just to Sam but to various situations throughout the series. We see this approach when Jamie Tartt struggles with public embarrassment after his reality TV appearance, when Roy Kent faces the difficulty of retirement, and when Rebecca deals with the aftermath of her divorce and revenge plot.

In Season 2, the goldfish philosophy is tested more severely when Ted himself struggles with panic attacks and psychological challenges. The show explores whether this approach to "letting go" is always healthy or whether some experiences require deeper processing and professional help. This adds complexity to the goldfish metaphor, showing that while it's valuable for everyday mistakes and setbacks, more significant trauma or persistent issues may require different approaches.

By Season 3, we see how various characters have internalized this philosophy in different ways. Some, like Sam, have learned to apply it effectively to maintain their mental health and performance. Others, like Nate, struggle with the balance between learning from mistakes and letting them go, showing that developing this skill takes time and practice.

The Balance Between Learning and Letting Go
One of the sophisticated aspects of Ted's goldfish advice is that it doesn't advocate for ignoring mistakes or avoiding accountability. Instead, it suggests a process: acknowledge the mistake, extract any useful learning, and then consciously choose to move forward without carrying the emotional weight of the error. This is evident in how Ted handles his own mistakes throughout the series. When he makes tactical errors or interpersonal missteps, he doesn't pretend they didn't happen or dismiss them as unimportant. He acknowledges them, makes appropriate amends or adjustments, and then demonstrates his own goldfish philosophy by not allowing past errors to paralyze his future decision-making.

The goldfish approach also prevents the perfectionism that can be so damaging to performance and well-being. By accepting that mistakes are inevitable and that the key skill is recovering from them quickly, Ted helps his players develop resilience and maintain the confidence necessary for peak performance.

Explanation

The ability to let go of past mistakes and approach each new moment with fresh perspective is one of the most crucial yet challenging skills for human well-being and performance. Our brains are evolutionarily wired to hold onto negative experiences more strongly than positive ones, a phenomenon psychologists call "negativity bias." This served our ancestors well when remembering dangers was essential for survival, but in modern life, this tendency often works against us. When we make mistakes, our minds naturally want to replay, analyze, and dwell on what went wrong. While some reflection can be valuable for learning, most of us far exceed the optimal amount of mistake-processing. We get caught in loops of rumination that increase anxiety, decrease confidence, and often lead to more mistakes as we become tense and overthinking.

The goldfish philosophy offers a different approach: rapid recovery and forward focus. This doesn't mean becoming careless or failing to learn from errors; rather, it involves developing the skill of efficient mistake processing. The sequence becomes: mistake happens, quickly extract any useful information, make any necessary corrections, and then consciously redirect attention to the present moment and future opportunities.

This approach is supported by extensive research in sports psychology and performance science. Athletes who can quickly "reset" after errors consistently outperform those who dwell on mistakes. The same principle applies to public speaking, creative work, relationships, and virtually any area where performance and well-being matter.

The goldfish metaphor is particularly powerful because it reframes our relationship with memory and past experience. Instead of seeing our ability to remember and replay negative experiences as always beneficial, it suggests that sometimes forgetting, or choosing not to dwell, is the healthier and more productive option. This philosophy also recognizes that mistakes are inevitable parts of growth and learning. When we approach errors with the expectation that we'll quickly move past them, we're more likely to take appropriate risks, try new approaches, and maintain the experimental mindset necessary for improvement and innovation.

The psychological benefits extend beyond performance. People who develop skill in letting go of minor mistakes and daily frustrations report higher levels of happiness, lower stress, and better relationships. They're less likely to carry grudges, more likely to forgive others' mistakes, and more resilient in the face of life's inevitable challenges.

However, the goldfish philosophy must be applied with wisdom and discernment. Not all negative experiences should be quickly forgotten—some require deeper processing, professional help, or significant life changes. The skill lies in distinguishing between everyday mistakes that benefit from quick release and more serious issues that need sustained attention and care.

Application

Try this four-step practice to develop your own goldfish-like resilience:

1. **Develop Mistake Recognition and Rapid Assessment:** When you make an error or experience a setback, practice immediate recognition without emotional escalation. Give yourself a specific time limit for this assessment, perhaps 2-3 minutes for minor mistakes, longer for more significant issues. The goal is to extract value from the experience without getting trapped in rumination cycles that serve no productive purpose.

2. **Practice the Mental Reset:** After your quick assessment, consciously choose to redirect your attention to the present moment and future opportunities. The key is making this a deliberate choice rather than hoping your mind will naturally move on.

3. **Reframe Your Relationship with Mistakes:** Work on seeing mistakes as information and learning opportunities rather than threats to your self-worth or competence.

4. **Build Goldfish Skills Gradually:** Start applying this philosophy to low-stakes mistakes and minor daily frustrations. As you develop skill with quick release and mental reset for small issues, you can gradually apply the same principles to larger setbacks and disappointments.

Remember that developing goldfish-like resilience is itself a skill that improves with practice. You won't master it immediately, and that's perfectly normal. Some mistakes will be easier to release than others, and your mental reset ability will be stronger on some days than on others. Additionally, note that this approach is most effective when combined with appropriate accountability and learning. The goal isn't to become careless or avoid responsibility, but to process mistakes efficiently and move forward productively rather than getting trapped in unproductive rumination.

Most importantly, extend this philosophy to how you respond to others' mistakes. When family members, colleagues, or friends make errors, help create an environment where people can acknowledge mistakes, learn what's useful, and then move forward without carrying unnecessary shame or anxiety. Your modeling of goldfish-like resilience gives others permission to do the same.

Takeaway

Every time you choose to let go of a mistake quickly and redirect your energy toward future opportunities, you build resilience and maintain the mental clarity necessary for peak performance and well-being. You also model for others what healthy mistake recovery looks like, creating environments where people can take appropriate risks and learn without fear of permanent judgment. The most successful and happiest people aren't those who never make mistakes. They're those who have developed the ability to recover from mistakes quickly and completely. They understand that dwelling on errors rarely produces additional value and often creates more problems than the original mistake did.

The next time you find yourself replaying a mistake or holding onto a frustration, remember Ted's goldfish wisdom and ask yourself: "What can I learn from this that will help me going forward?" Once you have that answer, make the conscious choice to be a goldfish. Let go of what's behind you and swim forward with fresh energy and clear focus.

After all, as Ted demonstrates throughout the series, the goal isn't to eliminate mistakes from your life; that's neither possible nor desirable if you want to keep growing and taking appropriate risks. The goal is to develop the resilience and mental agility that allow you to learn from errors without being defined or paralyzed by them.

Be a goldfish. Your happiness and success may depend on it.

Lesson #9:
Value Hard Lessons

The Example:

> Ted's quote: *"Taking on a challenge is a lot like riding a horse, isn't it? If you're comfortable while you're doing it, you're probably doing it wrong."*
>
> --- Ted Lasso, Season 1, Episode 1: "Pilot"

This profound observation comes early in Ted's journey, delivered during his first day at AFC Richmond as he and Coach Beard explore their new environment and prepare to take on what seems like an impossible challenge. The quote perfectly encapsulates one of Ted's core philosophies: that growth requires discomfort, and that the most valuable lessons often come wrapped in our most difficult experiences.

Context
- Ted's quote is delivered in the pilot episode as Ted arrives in England to begin coaching AFC Richmond, a sport and culture entirely new to him.
- The line comes as Ted Lasso is introduced to the daunting task of managing an English Premier League soccer team despite his lack of experience with the sport and little understanding of British football traditions.
- Rebecca Welton, club owner, intentionally hired Ted as part of a scheme to sabotage the team in retaliation against her ex-husband, but Ted is unaware of this and faces skepticism, ridicule, and doubt from staff, players, and fans.

- Ted uses this analogy to address both himself and those around him, acknowledging the discomfort and uncertainty inherent in taking on new, challenging roles.
- The horse metaphor sets a thematic tone for the entire series: growth comes from tackling difficult challenges, and true progress often requires stretching beyond one's comfort zone.

Audiences and critics have embraced the quote as a distillation of Ted's philosophy: that discomfort and vulnerability signal genuine effort and change, encouraging others to persist even when the path is unfamiliar or intimidating.

The horse-riding metaphor is particularly apt because it captures the essence of what makes challenges valuable. When you're learning to ride a horse, comfort is actually a warning sign. It means you're not pushing your limits, not developing new skills, and not building the muscle memory that comes from navigating uncertainty. A comfortable rider is either not riding at all, or riding so cautiously that they're not truly engaged with the dynamic, unpredictable nature of working with a powerful animal that has its own will and agenda.

Ted's Embodiment of the Philosophy

Ted doesn't just speak this philosophy; he lives it throughout the entire series. His decision to accept the Richmond job is itself a perfect example. He's an American football coach with zero soccer experience, taking on a Premier League team in a country where he knows virtually no one and understands little about the culture. By any reasonable measure, he should be terrified and overwhelmed. And he is, but he embraces that discomfort as a sign that he's exactly where he needs to be to grow.

From the very first episode, Ted demonstrates how to extract value from uncomfortable situations. During his surprise press conference, instead of being defensive about his lack of soccer knowledge, he uses self-deprecating humor to disarm hostile journalists. When Roy Kent dismisses him as "Ronald fucking McDonald," Ted doesn't retreat into hurt feelings but instead sees it as valuable information about what he needs to prove and how he needs to connect with his captain.

Season 1: Learning Through Professional Discomfort

Throughout Season 1, Ted consistently turns professional challenges into learning opportunities. When the team faces their first match in Episode 2, and the fans are openly hostile, Ted doesn't try to avoid the discomfort of their disapproval. Instead, he studies what their reactions tell him about the team's history, their expectations, and what he needs to do to earn their respect.

The relegation storyline provides perhaps the most powerful example of valuing hard lessons. In Season 1, Episode 10 ("The Hope That Kills You"), when Richmond faces Manchester City in the match that will determine their fate, Ted doesn't shy away from the enormous pressure and very real possibility of failure. Instead, he embraces the challenge as an opportunity for the team to discover what they're truly capable of under extreme pressure. Even when they ultimately lose and face relegation, one of the most devastating outcomes possible in professional soccer, Ted treats it as a valuable lesson rather than just a failure. He helps his players understand that their response to this setback will define them more than the setback itself.

Season 2: Deeper Discomfort, Deeper Growth

Season 2 takes this philosophy even further, particularly in Episode 1 ("Goodbye Earl") and throughout the season as Ted deals with increasingly complex psychological and emotional challenges. The introduction of Dr. Sharon Fieldstone, the sports psychologist, creates a different kind of discomfort for Ted, one that forces him to confront his own mental health struggles and his resistance to therapy. Ted's panic attacks represent the ultimate test of his "value hard lessons" philosophy. These aren't just professional challenges or tactical problems he can solve with optimism and folksy wisdom. They're deeply personal, frightening experiences that threaten his sense of control and competence. Yet even here, Ted gradually learns to see these episodes as valuable, though painful, information about his psychological state and what he needs to address to become healthier.

The Season 2 FA Cup semifinal against Manchester City (Episode 8: "Man City") provides another crucial example. The 5-0 defeat is not just a loss but a complete tactical and emotional breakdown. Jamie Tartt's personal crisis, the team's humiliation, and Ted's own sense of helplessness create a perfect storm of discomfort. Yet this devastating experience ultimately becomes the catalyst for important growth—for Jamie's reconciliation with his past, for the team's understanding of resilience, and for Ted's own journey toward getting professional help.

Season 3: Mastery Through Continued Challenge
In Season 3, we see Ted's philosophy fully matured as he faces perhaps his most challenging lesson: learning when to let go. His eventual decision to return to Kansas and leave Richmond isn't comfortable. It requires him to acknowledge that sometimes growth means stepping away from something good to pursue something necessary.

The season also shows how Ted has taught others to value hard lessons. Roy Kent's journey from player to coach requires him to embrace the discomfort of leadership and vulnerability. Nate's redemption arc involves facing the uncomfortable truth about his behavior and making amends. Rebecca's growth involves confronting her own patterns in relationships and her fears about being truly known and loved.

Explanation

The human tendency to avoid discomfort is so fundamental that it operates below the level of conscious thought. From birth, we're wired to seek pleasure and avoid pain, to move toward what feels safe and away from what feels threatening. This survival mechanism served our ancestors well when the primary threats were physical and immediate, but in our modern world, it often prevents us from accessing the very experiences that would help us grow and thrive. The problem with comfort-seeking as a life strategy is that it creates a downward spiral of diminishing capacity. When we consistently choose the easy path, we gradually lose our ability to handle difficulty. Our tolerance for uncertainty decreases, our resilience weakens, and our confidence erodes because we have fewer and fewer experiences of successfully navigating challenges.

Ted's horse-riding metaphor illuminates this perfectly. A rider who never pushes beyond their comfort zone never develops the deep balance, quick reflexes, and intuitive connection with the horse that comes from navigating unpredictable situations. They might feel safer in the short term, but they're actually more vulnerable because they haven't developed the skills necessary to handle unexpected challenges. The counterintuitive truth that Ted embodies is that discomfort is often a signal that we're in exactly the right place for growth. When we feel challenged, uncertain, or slightly overwhelmed, it usually means we're encountering situations that require us to develop new capabilities, think in different ways, or discover resources we didn't know we had.

This doesn't mean that all discomfort is valuable or that we should seek out suffering for its own sake. The key distinction is between productive discomfort, the kind that comes from stretching beyond our current limits in service of growth, and destructive discomfort that comes from harmful situations or relationships that damage rather than develop us.

Productive discomfort has several key characteristics: it's voluntary (we choose to engage with the challenge), it's purposeful (we understand why the difficulty might be valuable), it's finite (we know it won't last forever), and it's supported (we have resources and relationships to help us navigate it successfully). The psychological benefits of embracing productive discomfort are profound. Each time we successfully navigate a challenging situation, we build what psychologists call "self-efficacy"—confidence in our ability to handle future difficulties. This creates a positive feedback loop where our willingness to take on challenges increases our capacity to handle them, which in turn increases our willingness to take on even greater challenges.

Perhaps most importantly, valuing hard lessons teaches us to reframe our relationship with failure and setbacks. Instead of seeing difficulties as evidence of our inadequacy or signs that we should quit, we learn to see them as information about what we need to develop, evidence of our willingness to take risks, and proof that we're operating at the edge of our abilities where real growth occurs.

The alternative, organizing our lives around avoiding discomfort, ultimately leads to a kind of psychological atrophy. We become like muscles that are never challenged and gradually lose their strength, or like immune systems that are never exposed to mild stressors and become hypersensitive to normal challenges.

Application

Try this three-step practice to help you value and learn from hard lessons:

1. **Reframe Discomfort as Information:** The next time you encounter a situation that makes you uncomfortable, pause and ask yourself: "What is this discomfort trying to tell me?" Instead of immediately trying to escape or avoid the feeling, treat it as valuable data about where you might need to grow, what skills you might need to develop, or what fears you might need to face.

2. **Seek Out Controlled Challenges:** Deliberately put yourself in situations that are challenging but manageable. This might mean taking on a project that stretches your skills, having a difficult conversation you've been avoiding, learning something completely new, or volunteering for assignments that push you beyond your current expertise. The key is to choose challenges that are demanding enough to promote growth but not so overwhelming that they create trauma or lasting harm.

3. **Extract Learning from Difficult Experiences:** After navigating any challenging situation, whether you chose it or it was imposed on you, take time to extract the lessons consciously.

Remember that developing comfort with discomfort is itself a skill that improves with practice. Start with smaller challenges and gradually work your way up to bigger ones as your confidence and capacity grow. Pay attention to the difference between the acute discomfort of growth and the chronic discomfort that signals something is fundamentally wrong. Also, understand that valuing hard lessons doesn't mean becoming a masochist or seeking out unnecessary suffering. The goal is to become someone who can extract wisdom and growth from difficult experiences that are inevitable parts of life, and who can voluntarily take on challenges that promote development rather than simply avoiding anything that feels uncomfortable.

Most importantly, recognize that your willingness to learn from hard lessons not only benefits you but creates positive ripple effects for everyone around you. When people see you handling challenges with grace and extracting value from difficult experiences, they're more likely to approach their own challenges with the same growth mindset.

Takeaway

Every time you choose to embrace a challenge rather than avoid it, to seek the lesson in a difficult experience rather than just endure it, you build your capacity to handle whatever life brings your way. You also model for others what it looks like to approach difficulty as an opportunity rather than simply an obstacle. The most profound growth in your life has likely come not from your easiest moments but from your most challenging ones—from times when you had to dig deep, develop new capabilities, and discover resources you didn't know you possessed. These experiences, however uncomfortable they were at the time, became the foundation for your current strength, wisdom, and resilience.

The next time you find yourself facing a situation that makes you uncomfortable, remember Ted's horse-riding wisdom and ask yourself: "What if this discomfort is exactly where I need to be to grow? What if the fact that this feels challenging is a sign that I'm in the right place?" "What might I learn about myself if I stay curious and engaged rather than trying to escape as quickly as possible?"

After all, as Ted consistently demonstrates throughout the series, the goal isn't to eliminate discomfort from your life—that's neither possible nor desirable. The goal is to develop the mindset and skills that allow you to find value in inevitable challenges and to take on the difficulties that promote growth voluntarily. When you can do that, you transform from someone who is simply surviving life's hardships to someone who is actively using them as raw material for becoming the best version of yourself.

Taking on challenges is indeed a lot like riding a horse. If you're too comfortable, you're probably not really riding. But when you learn to find your balance in the discomfort, to stay curious and engaged even when things get unpredictable, that's when you discover what you're truly capable of.

Lesson #10:
Don't Settle for "Fine"

The Example:

> Roy's quote: "*You deserve someone who makes you feel like you've been struck by fucking lightning. Don't you dare settle for 'fine.'*"
>
> --- Roy Kent to Rebecca, Season 2, Episode 1: "Goodbye Earl"

Not all the lessons come from Ted. In one of the most emotionally charged and memorable moments of Ted Lasso's second season, Roy Kent delivers a passionate speech that cuts straight to the heart of what it means to live rather than merely exist truly. The scene takes place after a double dinner date where Rebecca introduces Roy and Keeley to her new boyfriend, John Wingsnight, a man who is perfectly adequate in every measurable way but utterly forgettable in every meaningful one.

When Rebecca asks for their opinion afterward, Keeley, ever the diplomatic friend, offers polite support, highlighting John's positive qualities while carefully avoiding any real enthusiasm. Roy, however, can no longer contain his frustration. His response erupts with the force of someone who has watched too many people settle for less than they deserve:

Context
- Rebecca is dating John Wingsnight, a delightful but unremarkable man.

- After a double date, Rebecca asks Roy and Keeley for their honest opinion about John.
- Keeley diplomatically focuses on John's positive qualities; he's age-appropriate, financially stable, and not shy.
- Roy becomes increasingly agitated by the conversation and Rebecca's apparent contentment with mediocrity.
- He finally explodes with his famous declaration about not settling for "fine".
- The moment represents Roy's core belief that life is too short and too precious to waste on anything less than extraordinary.

Roy's outburst isn't just about Rebecca's dating life; it's a manifesto about refusing to accept mediocrity in any form. He's a man who has spent his entire career pursuing excellence, who understands the difference between good and great, between acceptable and exceptional. He can't comprehend why anyone would willingly choose the mundane when the magnificent might be possible.

The phrase "struck by fucking lightning" is particularly powerful because lightning represents something sudden, overwhelming, and transformative. It's not gentle or predictable or safe; it's electric, dangerous, and utterly unmistakable. Roy is essentially arguing that love, real love, should feel like a force of nature, not like a pleasant afternoon stroll.

What makes this moment so compelling isn't just Roy's passionate delivery (though Brett Goldstein's performance is magnificent), but the underlying truth he's articulating. In a world that often encourages us to be practical, to settle, to be grateful for what we have, Roy is making the radical argument that we deserve more than just "fine." This scene also reveals Roy's own character development. Despite his gruff exterior and seeming cynicism, he's actually a romantic at heart, someone who believes deeply in the possibility of extraordinary connection. His relationship with Keeley exemplifies this philosophy; theirs is a partnership that defies conventional logic but creates something electric and transformative for both of them.

The moment has become iconic precisely because it speaks to a universal experience: the temptation to settle for safety over possibility, for comfort over passion, for "fine" over phenomenal. Roy's words serve as a wake-up call, challenging not just Rebecca but every viewer to examine their own lives and ask whether they're accepting mediocrity where they could be demanding magic.

Explanation

Roy's passionate plea to Rebecca reveals a fundamental truth about human nature: we have an alarming tendency to settle for "fine" in virtually every area of our lives. We accept jobs that pay the bills but drain our souls. We maintain friendships that are pleasant but superficial. We pursue goals that are achievable but uninspiring. And yes, we sometimes choose relationships that are comfortable but lack the spark that makes life feel truly alive. This pattern of settling isn't usually the result of a single conscious decision. Instead, it's the gradual accumulation of small compromises, practical considerations, and the quiet voice that whispers, "This is good enough." We convince ourselves that expecting more is unrealistic, selfish, or ungrateful. We tell ourselves that passion fades anyway, that stability matters more than excitement, that we should be practical about our expectations.

But Roy's outburst challenges this entire framework. He's essentially arguing that "fine" is not an acceptable standard for anything that truly matters in life. His use of the lightning metaphor is particularly significant—lightning doesn't ask permission, doesn't arrive on schedule, and can't be manufactured through careful planning. It's a force that transforms whatever it touches, leaving nothing unchanged.

The problem with settling for "fine" isn't just that we miss out on better experiences. It's that we gradually train ourselves to expect less from life. We become comfortable with mediocrity, skilled at finding reasons why extraordinary isn't necessary or realistic. We develop what psychologists call "learned helplessness," a condition where we stop believing that better outcomes are possible, even when they are.

This mindset becomes especially dangerous because it feeds itself. When we expect less, we often receive less. When we stop chasing the lightning, we gradually forget it's even there.

Roy's philosophy isn't just about romantic relationships; it's about approaching life with a fundamental belief that extraordinary is possible and that we deserve nothing less. This doesn't mean being unrealistic or refusing to appreciate good things; it means maintaining high standards and refusing to let practical considerations completely override our deeper desires and needs.

Consider the difference between these approaches: settling for a job that provides an adequate income versus pursuing work that ignites your passion and utilizes your unique talents. Similarly, maintain friendships that are pleasant but surface-level versus investing in relationships that challenge you to grow and support you through difficulties. Accepting a romantic partner who checks all the boxes on paper versus waiting for someone who makes your heart race and your mind expand.

The "struck by lightning" standard isn't about perfection; it's about transformation. It's about choosing experiences, relationships, and opportunities that change you, that make you more than you were before, that leave you knowing you're fully alive. Lightning can be uncomfortable, unpredictable, even dangerous, but it's never boring, and it's never forgotten.

This philosophy requires courage because it means risking the comfortable in pursuit of the extraordinary. It means potentially facing periods of loneliness, uncertainty, or disappointment while you wait for or work toward something that truly excites you. It means developing the confidence to believe that you deserve more than just "fine."

Application

Try this four-step practice to help yourself stop settling for "fine" and start reaching for lightning:

1. **Conduct a "Fine" Audit:** Take honest inventory of the areas in your life where you might be settling for mediocrity. Ask

yourself: Where am I choosing "fine" over potentially phenomenal? This might include your career, relationships, living situation, health habits, creative pursuits, or personal goals.

2. **Identify Your Lightning Moments:** Reflect on times in your life when you felt truly energized, passionate, and fully engaged. What were you doing? Who were you with? What conditions created that sense of being "struck by lightning"? Don't dismiss these experiences as unrealistic; use them as a compass pointing toward what's possible.

3. **Challenge Your Settling Stories:** Examine the narratives you tell yourself about why "fine" is acceptable or why lightning isn't realistic for you. While some practical considerations are valid, many of these stories are self-imposed limitations that keep us trapped in mediocrity. Ask yourself: "What would I pursue if I truly believed I deserved to be struck by lightning?"

4. **Take Lightning-Seeking Action:** Identify one area where you're settling and take a concrete step toward something more extraordinary. This doesn't mean dramatically upending your life overnight, but it does mean moving beyond comfortable inaction. This might mean having an honest conversation about what's missing in your relationship, applying for a job that excites rather than just sustains you, ending a friendship that drains your energy, or pursuing a creative project that feels meaningful rather than just productive.

Remember that seeking lightning doesn't mean being unrealistic or ungrateful. It means refusing to let fear or habit keep you trapped in situations that don't honor your full potential. It means believing that your life is valuable enough to demand more than just adequate. Also, understand that lightning-level experiences often require patience and persistence. The goal isn't to abandon everything good in pursuit of perfect, but to gradually raise your standards and actively create conditions where extraordinary becomes possible. Sometimes this means leaving the merely fine to make space for the phenomenal. Sometimes it means investing more deeply in existing relationships or situations to unlock their hidden potential.

Most importantly, recognize that you have more power to create lightning-struck experiences than you might believe. You can choose to believe that you deserve more than just "fine" and act accordingly.

Takeaway

Every time you choose to pursue the extraordinary instead of settling for the merely adequate, you honor the full potential of your one precious life. You also give others permission to do the same, creating a ripple effect that elevates everyone around you.

Roy's passionate declaration isn't just about romantic relationships. It's about living with the fundamental belief that you deserve to be fully alive, fully engaged, and fully yourself. It's about refusing to let practical considerations completely override the deeper longings of your heart and soul.

The next time you find yourself tempted to settle for "fine," remember Roy's words and ask yourself: "What would it look like to wait for lightning? What would I pursue if I truly believed I deserved to feel struck by something extraordinary?" Don't let fear, habit, or other people's low expectations convince you that mediocrity is your destiny. After all, as Roy demonstrated with his own relationship with Keeley, the most extraordinary experiences often come from the most unexpected places. Lightning doesn't always strike where we expect it, but it only strikes those who are brave enough to stand in the storm rather than hiding in the safe, comfortable, utterly forgettable shelter of "fine."

Life is too short and too precious to settle for anything less than the lightning that makes you feel truly, magnificently alive.

Lesson #11:
Transform Impossible into I'm Possible

The Example:

Ted's quote: "*You say impossible, but all I hear is 'I'm possible.'*"

--- Ted Lasso, Season 2, Episode 11: "Midnight Train to Royston"

This wordplay comes during one of the most emotionally charged episodes of the series, as Ted faces some of his greatest personal and professional challenges. The timing of this quote is particularly significant. It's delivered not during a moment of easy optimism, but during a period when things genuinely seem impossible for multiple characters. Ted is dealing with his divorce, panic attacks, and the complexities of his relationship with Dr. Sharon Fieldstone, while the team faces their own seemingly insurmountable obstacles.

Context
- The episode, titled "Midnight Train to Royston," finds AFC Richmond facing rising uncertainty: critical team changes, leadership rifts, and personal turmoil, including Ted's struggles with anxiety and his ongoing journey in therapy.
- The club is also facing pressure from outsiders, particularly regarding the future of star player Sam, creating an atmosphere filled with difficult choices and self-doubt.

- Ted uses this quote to motivate and lift the spirits of those around him, mainly the team, which is grappling with obstacles that seem insurmountable.
- It exemplifies Ted's relentless optimism and playful spirit, transforming negative language ("impossible") into possibility and hope, and encouraging others to embrace challenges as opportunities for growth.
- The line is delivered as part of Ted's trademark encouragement: he faces overwhelming odds but reframes them into something empowering through wordplay, reinforcing the show's theme of faith, hope, and belief in one's own capacity for change.

Ted's quote captures his ability to inspire, even during moments of discomfort and transition, reminding everyone that possibility can be found even in statements of doubt and difficulty.

The quote represents more than clever wordplay; it embodies Ted's fundamental approach to reframing challenges. Rather than denying that situations are difficult or pretending obstacles don't exist, Ted consistently finds ways to shift perspective from limitation-focused thinking to possibility-focused thinking. This linguistic sleight of hand reveals a deeper truth about how the language we use shapes our reality and our capacity to find solutions.

The Context of Season 2's Deepest Challenges

By Episode 11 of Season 2, both Ted and his team are facing what appear to be truly impossible situations. Ted is grappling with his most serious personal challenges yet. His mental health struggles have become more pronounced, his marriage has definitively ended, and he's been forced to confront painful truths about his father's death and his own psychological patterns. The team, meanwhile, is dealing with their own complex dynamics. Jamie Tartt is working his way back into the squad after his humbling experiences, Roy Kent is navigating his transition from player to coach, and the club faces ongoing pressure to perform in the Premier League while dealing with internal conflicts and external skepticism.

In this context, Ted's "I'm possible" reframe isn't delivered from a place of naive optimism or easy confidence. It comes from someone who has looked directly at seemingly impossible circumstances and chosen to find ways to work within and through them rather than being paralyzed by their difficulty.

The Power of Linguistic Reframing

Ted's wordplay demonstrates something profound about how language shapes thought and action. When we label something "impossible," we essentially close off our mental pathways to solutions. The word itself suggests that no amount of effort, creativity, or persistence can overcome the obstacle. This linguistic framing often becomes a self-fulfilling prophecy, as we stop looking for possibilities that might actually exist.

By hearing "I'm possible" instead of "impossible," Ted models a cognitive technique that psychologists call "reframing," consciously choosing to interpret situations in ways that open up possibilities rather than closing them down. This isn't about denying reality or pretending that genuine obstacles don't exist, but rather about maintaining a mindset that continues to search for pathways forward. This reframing technique appears throughout Ted's interactions with his players and colleagues. When others see insurmountable problems, Ted consistently finds ways to highlight opportunities, potential solutions, or alternative perspectives that weren't initially obvious.

Applications Throughout the Series

We see Ted apply this "I'm possible" thinking in numerous situations across the series. When he first arrives at Richmond and everyone assumes an American football coach can't possibly succeed in English soccer, Ted doesn't argue against the difficulty of the challenge. Instead, he approaches it as an interesting problem to solve rather than an impossible barrier to overcome. With individual players, Ted consistently helps them reframe their self-limiting beliefs. When Jamie Tartt believes he's irredeemably selfish, Ted helps him see the possibility of growth and change. When Roy Kent feels that his playing career is definitely over, Ted helps him discover new possibilities in coaching and mentorship.

When Sam Obisanya faces pressure that seems to threaten his career and values, Ted supports him in finding creative solutions that honor both his principles and his opportunities.

The "I'm possible" philosophy is particularly evident in Ted's approach to mental health challenges. Rather than seeing his panic attacks as evidence that he's fundamentally broken or incapable, Ted gradually learns to view them as information about what he needs to address and heal. This reframe allows him to seek help and develop coping strategies rather than being defeated by his symptoms.

Season 3 and the Fruition of Possibility Thinking

By Season 3, we see how Ted's consistent "I'm possible" approach has created conditions for breakthrough moments that might have seemed impossible in earlier seasons. Characters who seemed permanently stuck in negative patterns find paths to growth and change. Relationships that appeared irreparably damaged discover possibilities for healing and renewal.

The culmination of this philosophy is perhaps most evident in the series finale, where multiple storylines that seemed to have impossible obstacles find creative resolutions. These aren't magical solutions but rather the natural result of characters who have learned to keep looking for possibilities even when conventional wisdom suggests none exist.

The Science Behind Possibility Thinking

Ted's reframing technique aligns with significant research in cognitive psychology and neuroscience. Studies show that our brains are constantly filtering the information available to us based on what we believe is possible or important. When we believe something is impossible, we literally stop noticing information that might lead to solutions. Conversely, when we maintain belief in possibilities, our brains continue to process information that might be relevant to achieving our goals. This phenomenon, known as "selective attention" or the "reticular activating system," means that possibility thinking creates more opportunities for breakthrough moments and creative solutions.

The "I'm possible" mindset also relates to what psychologists call a "growth mindset"—the belief that abilities and circumstances can be developed and changed through effort and learning. People with growth mindsets are more resilient in the face of obstacles, more likely to persist through difficulties, and more open to feedback and new approaches.

Explanation

The difference between seeing situations as impossible versus seeing them as opportunities to discover what's possible represents one of the most crucial distinctions in human psychology and achievement. This isn't merely about positive thinking or optimism. It's about how our fundamental assumptions about what can and cannot be done directly influence our ability to find solutions, maintain motivation, and persist through difficulties.

When we label something as impossible, we engage in what psychologists call "cognitive closure." We stop searching for additional information or alternative approaches because we've concluded that no solutions exist. This mental shortcut, while sometimes protective and realistic, often prevents us from discovering pathways that weren't immediately obvious but are actually available with creativity, persistence, or new information. The "I'm possible" reframe works because it keeps our minds actively engaged in solution-seeking rather than passively accepting limitations. This doesn't mean denying genuine obstacles or constraints, but rather maintaining the mental flexibility to continue exploring options even when initial approaches seem blocked.

This distinction becomes particularly important when facing complex, multifaceted challenges that don't have obvious solutions. Many of life's most significant problems—relationship difficulties, career transitions, health challenges, creative projects—require sustained effort and multiple approaches before breakthrough moments emerge. The "impossible" mindset tends to give up too early, while the "I'm possible" mindset maintains engagement long enough for creative solutions to develop. The reframing technique also influences how we interpret setbacks and failures. When we believe something is possible, temporary failures become information about what doesn't work rather than confirmation that success is impossible. This interpretation supports resilience and continued effort rather than discouragement and abandonment of goals.

Additionally, the language we use doesn't just reflect our thinking; it shapes it. When we consistently use possibility-focused language, we gradually retrain our brains to look for opportunities rather than obstacles, to notice resources rather than limitations, and to generate creative approaches rather than accepting constraints. The "I'm possible" philosophy also recognizes that many things that seem impossible are actually just difficult, unfamiliar, or requiring approaches we haven't yet discovered. Throughout history, countless "impossible" achievements have been accomplished by people who refused to accept initial assessments of impossibility and continued working toward solutions.

However, effective possibility thinking must be grounded in reality and accompanied by genuine effort. Simply changing language without taking corresponding action becomes meaningless optimism. The power of Ted's approach lies in combining the reframe with consistent work toward solutions, willingness to learn new approaches, and persistence through inevitable setbacks.

Application

Try this four-step practice to develop your own skill in transforming impossible into "I'm possible":

1. **Identify Your "Impossible" Beliefs:** Take inventory of areas in your life where you've concluded that change or improvement is impossible. These might include: "I'm not good with technology," "I could never start my own business," "My relationship with [person] will never improve," or "I'll never be able to [specific skill or achievement]." Recognize that these statements often reflect current limitations rather than permanent realities.

2. **Practice Linguistic Reframing:** For each "impossible" belief you've identified, experiment with possibility-focused

language. Instead of "I'm not good with technology," try "I'm developing my technology skills." Instead of "I could never start my own business," try "I'm exploring what it would take to start a business." Instead of "My relationship with [person] will never improve," try "I'm looking for ways to improve my relationship with [person]."

3. **Engage in Possibility Research:** For one area where you've been thinking "impossible," commit to actively researching what might actually be possible.

4. **Take "I'm Possible" Actions:** Choose one reframed belief and commit to taking small, concrete actions that align with the possibility rather than the impossibility. The key is taking actions that reinforce the possibility-focused mindset and generate new information about what might be achievable.

Remember that transforming impossible into "I'm possible" is a skill that develops over time. Start with smaller challenges where the reframe feels manageable and gradually apply it to larger obstacles as your confidence and ability grow. Also, understand that not every difficult situation will become easy through reframing, and some genuine limitations do exist. The value of possibility thinking lies not in guaranteeing specific outcomes but in maintaining the mental flexibility and motivation necessary to find creative solutions and pathways that weren't initially apparent.

Most importantly, combine possibility thinking with realistic assessment and genuine effort. The "I'm possible" mindset works best when it's supported by concrete actions, willingness to learn, and persistence through the inevitable challenges that arise when working toward difficult goals.

Takeaway

Every time you choose to hear "I'm possible" instead of "impossible," you keep your mind engaged in solution-seeking rather than accepting premature limitations. You also model for others what it looks like to maintain hope and creativity in the face of challenging circumstances.

The most significant breakthroughs in your life have likely come in areas where others—or even you yourself—initially thought success was impossible. Whether it's learning a new skill, overcoming a personal challenge, building a meaningful relationship, or achieving a professional goal, the transformation from "impossible" to accomplished often begins with the simple shift from limitation-focused to possibility-focused thinking.

The next time you catch yourself or someone else declaring something impossible, remember Ted's wordplay and ask: "What if this isn't impossible but just difficult in ways I haven't figured out yet?" "What would I try if I believed this was possible?" "Who might have insights about pathways I haven't considered?" After all, as Ted demonstrates throughout the series, many of the things that seem most impossible are simply waiting for someone with the right combination of possibility thinking, creative problem-solving, and persistent effort to unlock them. The question isn't whether impossible situations exist—they do. The question is whether you'll let the label of "impossible" stop you from discovering what might actually be possible with enough curiosity, creativity, and commitment.

You say impossible, but all you need to hear is "I'm possible." That simple reframe might be the beginning of your next breakthrough.

Lesson #12:
Find Strength in Shared Struggle

The Example:

Ted's quote: "*I promise you, there is something worse out there than being sad — and that is being alone and being sad. Ain't nobody in this room alone.*"

--- Ted Lasso to his team, Season 1, Episode 10: "The Hope That Kills You"

This powerful statement comes during one of the most emotionally devastating moments in the entire series—immediately after AFC Richmond's relegation to the Championship League. The team has just experienced what should have been their greatest triumph, tying Manchester City in the final seconds to avoid relegation, only to have that hope crushed by Jamie Tartt's last-second goal that sends them down to the second tier.

Context
Here's the context in this episode and across the series:
- Ted delivers this wisdom immediately after the team's most devastating loss, when isolation would be the natural response.
- The quote reframes collective disappointment as an opportunity for deeper connection rather than individual withdrawal.
- Ted distinguishes between unavoidable sadness and avoidable loneliness, focusing on what the team can control.

- The philosophy appears throughout the series as characters learn to process difficulties within supportive relationships.
- Ted models this approach in his own journey by eventually accepting help during his personal struggles.
- The lesson establishes that true community includes supporting each other through failures, not just celebrating successes together.

In this moment of collective heartbreak, when players are sitting in stunned silence, processing the magnitude of their failure, Ted doesn't try to minimize their pain or offer false optimism about silver linings. Instead, he acknowledges the reality of their sadness while reframing it as a shared experience that, paradoxically, makes them less alone than they might feel in their individual disappointment.

The timing of this quote is crucial. It comes not during a motivational pep talk before a big game, but in the immediate aftermath of devastating defeat. Ted's words offer comfort not by denying the pain but by transforming it from an isolating experience into a connecting one. He's essentially teaching his players (and viewers) that while we cannot always control what happens to us, we can choose how we process difficult experiences—alone or together.

The Context of Devastating Collective Loss
"The Hope That Kills You" represents the culmination of an entire season's worth of struggle, growth, and ultimately heartbreak. The episode title itself references the cruel nature of hope, how believing in positive outcomes can make eventual disappointment even more painful. But Ted's response to this "hope that kills you" offers a different perspective: shared pain is more bearable than solitary pain.

The locker room scene where Ted delivers these words is one of the series' most emotionally raw moments. Players who have spent the season learning to function as a team are now facing the consequences of collective failure. Each individual could retreat into private shame, personal regret, or individual blame. Instead,

Ted helps them understand that their shared disappointment can become a source of connection rather than isolation.

This moment also represents Ted's most profound teaching about the nature of community and resilience. He's not offering a quick fix or trying to make the players feel better immediately. Instead, he's providing a framework for processing difficult emotions in a way that strengthens rather than weakens their bonds with each other.

The Psychology of Shared Suffering

Ted's insight reflects deep psychological truths about human connection and emotional processing. Research in psychology consistently shows that people who process difficult experiences in supportive social contexts recover more quickly and completely than those who face challenges alone. This isn't just about having people to talk to—it's about the fundamental human need to feel understood and connected, especially during our most vulnerable moments.

The quote distinguishes between two different types of emotional pain: sadness itself and sadness compounded by isolation. Ted recognizes that while the team cannot avoid feeling disappointed about their relegation, they can avoid the additional suffering that comes from bearing that disappointment alone. This distinction is crucial because it identifies an element of their experience that they can actually control. When people face setbacks alone, they often engage in rumination, self-blame, and catastrophic thinking that can spiral into depression or hopelessness. But when the same setbacks are experienced within a supportive community, the emotional processing becomes more balanced, realistic, and ultimately healing. Others can provide perspective, share the emotional burden, and remind us that our worst moments don't define our entire worth or future.

The Power of "Ain't Nobody in This Room Alone"

The second part of Ted's statement—"Ain't nobody in this room alone"—transforms the entire emotional landscape of the moment. With these words, he shifts each player's focus from their individual disappointment to their collective support system. He's reminding them that they're not just teammates who happen to be sad at the same time; they're people who can help each other carry the weight of this shared disappointment.

This declaration also serves as both a statement of fact and a commitment. Ted is observing that they are literally not alone in that moment, but he's also promising that the team will continue to support each other through the processing of this setback. He's establishing that their community will persist beyond this moment of crisis. The phrase also reflects Ted's understanding that isolation is often a choice we make when we're hurting, not just a circumstance that happens to us. People in pain frequently withdraw from others, if no one else could understand their specific disappointment or that their sadness would burden others. Ted preemptively counters this tendency by explicitly stating that they are not alone and implicitly encouraging them not to make themselves alone through withdrawal.

Applications Throughout the Series
This philosophy of shared struggle creating connection rather than division appears throughout Ted Lasso in various forms. When characters face personal challenges: Ted's panic attacks, Roy's retirement, Rebecca's divorce aftermath, Jamie's family issues—the show consistently demonstrates that healing happens most effectively within supportive relationships rather than through isolated self-reliance.

The concept also applies to how the team handles future setbacks and challenges. Having learned to process their relegation collectively, the players develop resilience that serves them in subsequent difficulties. They understand that setbacks don't have to be isolating experiences and that their team identity includes supporting each other through tough times, not just celebrating together during good times.

Ted himself models this philosophy throughout the series. When he faces personal challenges, his eventual healing comes not through hiding his struggles but through accepting support from Dr. Sharon Fieldstone, Coach Beard, and others who care about him. His journey demonstrates that even the person who typically provides support for others needs community during difficult times.

The Broader Implications for Community Building

Ted's approach to handling collective disappointment provides a template for building resilient communities, whether in sports, workplaces, families, or other group contexts. Instead of allowing setbacks to fragment the group—with individuals retreating into private blame or disappointment—effective leaders help groups process difficulties together in ways that strengthen rather than weaken their bonds. This requires creating psychological safety where people feel comfortable being vulnerable about their disappointments and fears. It also requires reframing setbacks as shared experiences rather than individual failures, even when some team members may bear more responsibility than others for particular outcomes.

The philosophy also recognizes that community isn't just valuable during good times—it's essential during difficult times. Groups that only celebrate together but don't support each other through challenges tend to be fair-weather communities that fragment when real tests arise. Ted is essentially teaching his team that their strength as a group will be measured not by how they handle success but by how they support each other through failure.

Explanation

The human tendency to withdraw and isolate during times of emotional pain represents one of our most counterproductive yet understandable responses to suffering. When we're disappointed, embarrassed, or grieving, our instinct is often to retreat from others, assuming that our pain is too personal to share or that others couldn't possibly understand our specific situation. Ted's wisdom directly challenges this tendency by distinguishing between the unavoidable pain of difficult experiences and the additional, unnecessary suffering that comes from facing those experiences alone.

This insight reflects fundamental truths about human psychology and social connection. Humans are inherently social creatures who have evolved to survive and thrive in groups. Our emotional and psychological well-being is deeply connected to our sense of belonging and social support. When we face challenges in isolation, we're working against our basic psychological architecture, making recovery more difficult and incomplete. Research in psychology and neuroscience shows that social connection activates the same reward pathways in the brain as food, water, and other basic needs. Conversely, social isolation triggers the same threat-detection systems as physical pain. This means that when Ted tells his players they're not alone, he's not just offering emotional comfort— he's addressing a fundamental neurological need that affects their capacity to process and recover from disappointment.

The distinction Ted makes between being sad and being alone while sad is particularly important because it identifies an element of suffering that we can actually control. While we cannot always prevent disappointments, setbacks, or losses from occurring, we can choose how we process these experiences. We can face them within supportive relationships that help us maintain perspective and find meaning, or we can face them alone in ways that amplify the pain and delay recovery. Shared suffering also creates what psychologists call "post-traumatic growth", the phenomenon where people who process difficult experiences together often emerge stronger and more connected than they were before the challenge occurred. This happens because working through difficulties together builds trust, reveals character, and creates deeper bonds than are possible through shared positive experiences alone.

Ted's approach also recognizes that isolation during difficult times often stems from shame, the belief that our failures or disappointments reflect fundamental flaws that others would judge harshly if they knew the truth. By explicitly stating that no one is alone in their disappointment, Ted counters the shame response that typically drives people to withdraw during their most vulnerable moments.

Furthermore, the philosophy acknowledges that community isn't just about individual comfort. It's about collective resilience. Groups that learn to support each other through setbacks develop the kind of trust and solidarity that makes them stronger and more effective over time. They understand that everyone will face difficulties and that mutual support isn't just kindness—it's practical wisdom that benefits everyone in the long run.

Application

Try this three-step practice to build and maintain a supportive community during difficult times:

1. **Recognize the Isolation Impulse:** When you face disappointments, failures, or emotional pain, notice your natural tendency to withdraw from others and handle the situation alone. Before retreating completely, consider whether sharing your struggle with trusted friends, family members, or colleagues might provide perspective and support that helps you recover more effectively.

2. **Reframe Setbacks as Shared Learning Opportunities:** When your group, team, or family faces collective disappointments, help reframe these experiences as opportunities to strengthen relationships rather than reasons for individual withdrawal or blame. Focus on processing the experience collectively rather than allowing people to retreat into private shame or individual problem-solving that fragments the group's mutual support.

3. **Practice Being Present for Others' Pain:** Develop your capacity to sit with others during their difficult moments without trying to fix, minimize, or rush past their pain. Sometimes the most powerful support you can offer is simply being present and reminding someone that they don't have to face their struggles alone.

Remember that building a supportive community is an ongoing process that requires consistent attention and effort from everyone involved. Some people may be more comfortable sharing struggles than others, and it's important to respect individual differences while still encouraging connection and mutual support. Also, understand that being part of a supportive community means both giving and receiving help, sometimes on the same day.

Most importantly, recognize that admitting you need support during difficult times isn't a sign of weakness; it's a sign of wisdom and emotional intelligence. The strongest and most resilient people are typically those who have learned to leverage social support during challenging periods rather than trying to handle everything alone.

Takeaway

Every time you choose to face difficulties within supportive relationships rather than in isolation, you not only improve your own capacity to recover and grow but also strengthen the bonds that make real community possible. You also model for others what it looks like to seek and offer support during tough times, creating permission for mutual vulnerability and care. The most resilient people and communities aren't those who never face setbacks. They're those who have learned to process difficulties together in ways that strengthen rather than weaken their connections. They understand that shared sadness is more bearable than isolated sadness and that supporting each other through failures builds the trust and solidarity necessary for long-term success and well-being.

The next time you face disappointment or emotional pain, remember Ted's wisdom and ask yourself: "How can I process this experience in connection with others rather than alone?" "Who in my life might benefit from knowing they're not the only one facing this type of challenge?"

After all, as Ted demonstrates in that devastating locker room moment, some of our deepest connections are forged not during our happiest times but during our most difficult ones, when we choose to face our pain together rather than apart. There is indeed something worse than being sad—and that's being alone while you're sad. But the beautiful truth is that you don't have to be alone, because ain't nobody in this room, or in your life, who has to face their struggles in isolation.

Find strength in shared struggle. It's one of humanity's greatest resources.

Lesson #13:
Trust Your Moral Compass

The Example:

Ted's quote: "*Doing the right thing is never the wrong thing.*"

--- Ted Lasso, Season 2, Episode 3: "Do the Right-est Thing"

This deceptively simple statement comes during an episode that grapples with complex moral dilemmas and the challenges of maintaining ethical standards in a world that often rewards compromise. The episode title itself, "Do the Right-est Thing," playfully acknowledges that figuring out what's "right" isn't always straightforward. Still, Ted's quote provides clarity: when you can identify the right thing to do, you should do it, regardless of the potential costs or complications.

Context

Here's the context in this episode and across the series:
- Ted delivers this wisdom during an episode focused on complex moral dilemmas and ethical decision-making.
- The quote provides clarity and simplicity in situations where moral relativism might create confusion or paralysis.
- Multiple characters throughout the series demonstrate this principle by choosing integrity over expedience.
- The philosophy emphasizes moral courage and the willingness to accept short-term costs for long-term integrity.

- Ted models this approach by consistently aligning his actions with his values, even when it's difficult or costly.
- The series shows that moral compromise often creates more problems than it solves, while ethical consistency builds trust and self-respect.

The timing of this wisdom in Season 2, Episode 3 is significant as it occurs during a period when multiple characters are facing ethical crossroads. Ted is dealing with the complexities of coaching while managing his own mental health challenges, Rebecca is navigating her relationship with Sam despite the obvious complications, and the team is learning to balance individual desires with collective responsibilities.

Ted's statement serves as both a personal philosophy and a leadership principle. It reflects his belief that moral clarity, while sometimes challenging to achieve, should guide decision-making even when the right choice seems disadvantageous in the short term. This isn't naive idealism; Ted understands that doing the right thing often comes with costs, but rather a mature recognition that integrity and long-term well-being require consistency between values and actions.

The Context of Complex Moral Decisions

"Do the Right-est Thing" presents several storylines where characters must navigate the gap between what's easy, what's advantageous, and what's right. The episode explores how good people can face genuinely difficult ethical dilemmas where the "right" choice isn't immediately obvious, but once moral clarity emerges, the path forward becomes clear, even if it's not easy.

Ted's quote comes at a moment when he's advising someone (the specific context varies depending on the scene, but the principle remains constant) who is struggling with a decision that pits short-term convenience against long-term integrity. Rather than offering complex ethical analysis or situational reasoning, Ted provides this straightforward moral framework: when you know what's right, that knowledge should guide your action. This philosophy reflects Ted's broader approach to leadership and life. He believes that most people have good instincts about right and wrong, but they sometimes need permission or encouragement to act on those instincts when external pressures suggest alternative courses of action. His role, as he sees it, is to create environments where people feel safe to do the right thing even when it's difficult.

The Simplicity and Power of Moral Clarity

Ted's statement cuts through the complexity that often surrounds ethical decision-making in modern life. We live in a world where moral relativism, situational ethics, and pragmatic compromise are often presented as sophisticated approaches to difficult decisions. While these frameworks can be useful for analyzing complex situations, they can also create paralysis or provide justification for choices that we intuitively know are wrong.

"Doing the right thing is never the wrong thing" offers a different approach: trust your moral instincts, act with integrity, and accept that short-term costs are often the price of long-term peace of mind and authentic relationships. This doesn't mean that identifying the "right thing" is always easy. Sometimes it requires careful thought, consultation with others, and honest self-examination, but once that clarity emerges, action becomes straightforward.

The power of this philosophy lies in its recognition that moral compromise, while sometimes seeming practical or necessary, often creates more problems than it solves. When we act against our better judgment or violate our core values for short-term advantage, we typically end up with damaged relationships, internal conflict, and situations that become more complicated rather than less.

Applications Throughout the Series

This principle appears throughout in both explicit and implicit forms as characters face moments where they must choose between expedience and ethics. Rebecca's eventual honesty about her revenge plot against Ted represents a "doing the right thing" moment—confessing was difficult and potentially costly, but it ultimately strengthened her relationships and freed her from the burden of deception.

Roy's decision to retire when he realized his declining abilities were hurting the team exemplifies this philosophy. He could have continued playing, holding onto his position and salary, but he recognized that stepping aside was the right thing for everyone involved, even though it meant giving up his identity as an active player.

Jamie's choice to return to Richmond and work on his character represents another application of this principle. The easier path would have been to stay at Manchester City or continue his reality TV pursuits, but he recognized that personal growth required him to face his past mistakes and make amends with the people he had hurt.

Even Ted's decision to seek help from Dr. Sharon Fieldstone, despite his initial resistance to therapy, demonstrates this principle. Admitting he needed help wasn't easy for someone who had built his identity around helping others, but he recognized that getting support was the right thing for his mental health and his effectiveness as a coach.

The Challenge of Moral Courage
While Ted's quote sounds simple, applying it requires what philosophers call "moral courage", the willingness to act on your ethical convictions even when doing so is difficult, costly, or unpopular. This type of courage is often more challenging than physical bravery because it requires sustained commitment to principles rather than momentary heroic action.

The series demonstrates that moral courage often entails sacrifice: Rebecca relinquishes her desire for revenge, Roy forgoes his career as a player, Jamie sacrifices his ego protection, and Ted relinquishes his preference for handling everything alone. These sacrifices aren't trivial, but the characters discover that the alternative, compromising their values, ultimately costs them more in terms of self-respect, relationships, and peace of mind.

Ted's philosophy also recognizes that doing the right thing often creates short-term complications while preventing long-term problems. Honesty might hurt feelings in the moment, but it prevents the greater damage that comes from deception. Taking responsibility might be embarrassing initially, but it builds trust and credibility over time. Standing up for principles might create conflict temporarily, but it establishes boundaries and earns respect ultimately.

The Relationship Between Values and Actions

The quote reflects a fundamental truth about psychological well-being and authentic living: alignment between our values and our actions is essential for mental health, self-respect, and meaningful relationships. When we consistently act against our better judgment or violate our core principles, we create internal conflict and cognitive dissonance that undermines our overall well-being.

Ted's approach suggests that most people already know what the right thing is in most situations. The challenge isn't figuring out right from wrong but finding the courage to act on that knowledge when external pressures suggest otherwise. This emphasizes character development and moral courage rather than complex ethical reasoning.

The philosophy also implies that "wrong" outcomes resulting from right actions are ultimately less damaging than "right" outcomes achieved through wrong actions. A person who loses a job for refusing to compromise their ethics is in a better long-term position than someone who keeps their job through deception or betrayal of their values.

Explanation

The struggle between doing what is right and doing what is easy, profitable, or socially acceptable is one of the core challenges of human life. Ted's seemingly straightforward statement: "doing the right thing is never the wrong thing," addresses this challenge by providing a clear decision-making guide that values moral integrity over convenience.

This philosophy runs counter to much of modern ethical thinking, which often emphasizes context, complexity, and nuanced analysis of competing interests. While such approaches can be valuable for understanding difficult situations, they can also create paralysis or provide intellectual justification for choices that we intuitively recognize as wrong. Ted's approach suggests that moral truth, while sometimes difficult to discern, becomes a reliable guide for action once identified.

The psychological research on moral decision-making supports Ted's insight in several important ways. Studies show that people who consistently act in accordance with their stated values report higher levels of life satisfaction, better relationships, and greater resilience in the face of adversity. Conversely, people who frequently compromise their principles experience increased anxiety, depression, and interpersonal difficulties. This occurs because humans have a fundamental need for coherence between their beliefs and their actions.

Ted's philosophy prevents this downward spiral by establishing a clear priority: when you know what's right, do it, regardless of the immediate costs. This approach maintains the integrity of both our moral framework and our self-concept, even when external circumstances make right action difficult or costly.

The quote also reflects an understanding of the long-term consequences of moral choices. While doing the right thing might create short-term difficulties, honest feedback might hurt someone's feelings, standing up to a bully might invite retaliation, and admitting mistakes might damage our reputation. These temporary costs are typically far less damaging than the long-term consequences of moral compromise. When we act unethically, we often create problems that compound over time: lies require more lies to sustain them, betrayals damage trust that can be difficult or impossible to rebuild, and shortcuts based on moral compromise often lead to dead ends or further ethical dilemmas. Ted's approach recognizes that accepting the immediate costs of right action is almost always preferable to dealing with the accumulated costs of wrong action.

The philosophy also acknowledges that moral clarity, while sometimes challenging to achieve, is usually possible for people who are willing to be honest with themselves about their values and the likely consequences of their choices. Most ethical dilemmas aren't actually that complex once we strip away self-serving rationalizations and focus on fundamental questions: What would happen if everyone acted this way? How would I feel if I were on the receiving end of this action? What choice would I be proud to explain to someone I respect?

Application

Try this four-step practice to align your actions with your values consistently:

1. **Clarify Your Core Values and Moral Principles:** Take time to identify and articulate the values that are most important to you—things like honesty, fairness, compassion, integrity, or loyalty.

2. **Develop "Right Thing" Recognition Skills:** Practice identifying moments when you face choices between what's right and what's easy, advantageous, or socially acceptable. These might include opportunities to take credit for others' work, moments when you could lie to avoid consequences, situations where you witness unfair treatment, or times when keeping a commitment becomes inconvenient.

3. **Build Moral Courage Gradually:** Start by doing the right thing in low-stakes situations to build your confidence and moral muscle for bigger challenges. As you experience the positive long-term effects of ethical behavior in small matters, you'll develop the courage and conviction necessary for more significant moral challenges.

4. **Accept Short-term Costs for Long-term Integrity:** When you identify the right thing to do, commit to accepting whatever immediate costs or complications might result from that choice. Focus on the long-term benefits of maintaining your integrity: better relationships based on trust, improved self-respect, and the peace of mind that comes from knowing your actions align with your values.

Remember that doing the right thing doesn't mean being rigid, judgmental, or unable to consider context and nuance. It means having clear principles that guide your behavior while remaining open to learning and growth. Sometimes new information or perspectives will help you better understand what the "right thing" actually is, and wisdom includes the flexibility to adjust your actions when your understanding improves. Also, understand that doing the right thing doesn't guarantee immediate positive outcomes or universal approval. Sometimes, right actions are misunderstood, unappreciated, or even punished in the short term. The value lies not in external validation but in maintaining alignment between your values and your behavior, which is the foundation of authentic self-respect and meaningful relationships.

Takeaway

Every day presents you with opportunities to choose between what's right and what's convenient, and these choices accumulate to define not only your character but also the quality of your relationships and your own sense of self-worth. While doing the right thing isn't always easy, it's always worth it in the long run.

The most respected and trusted people in any context aren't those who never face moral dilemmas, but those who consistently choose integrity when those dilemmas arise. They understand that reputation and relationships are built on a foundation of ethical consistency, and that no short-term advantage is worth compromising that foundation.

The next time you face a choice between what's right and what's easy, remember Ted's wisdom and ask yourself: "What's the right thing to do here?" "How will I feel about this choice in five years?"

After all, as Ted demonstrates throughout the series, moral complexity is often just an excuse for moral compromise. While figuring out the right thing to do can sometimes be challenging, actually doing it once you've figured it out is a choice that reveals your character and shapes your future.

Doing the right thing is never the wrong thing, even when it's hard, especially when it's hard.

Lesson #14:
Stay Present and Take Action

The Example:

Ted's quote: *"There's two buttons I never like hittin', and that's panic and snooze."*

--- Ted Lasso, Season 2, Episode 1: "Goodbye Earl"

This clever metaphor comes at the beginning of Season 2, setting the tone for Ted's approach to handling the new challenges that await AFC Richmond in their Championship League campaign. The timing is significant. Ted delivers this wisdom as the team prepares for their first season after relegation. This period could easily trigger both panic about their reduced status and a temptation to coast or hit the metaphorical snooze button on their ambitions.

Context
Here's the context in this episode and across the series:
- Ted delivers this wisdom at the beginning of Season 2 as the team faces the challenges of relegation and Championship League competition.
- The quote provides a framework for avoiding both frantic overreaction and passive avoidance when facing difficulties.
- Ted models this approach throughout Season 2 as he deals with mental health challenges, divorce, and professional pressure.
- Multiple characters demonstrate the effectiveness of this middle path by staying engaged with their challenges without being overwhelmed.

- The philosophy applies to both crisis management and everyday decision-making, advocating for present, measured action.
- The series shows that both panic and avoidance typically create more problems than they solve, while calm engagement leads to better outcomes.

Ted's comparison of panic and snooze buttons reveals his understanding that both responses, frantic overreaction and passive avoidance, are counterproductive ways of dealing with challenges. Whether we're facing setbacks, new responsibilities, or uncertain situations, Ted suggests that the most effective approach lies between these two extremes: staying calm and engaged, present and active.

The Context of Season 2's New Challenges
"Goodbye Earl" opens with AFC Richmond facing the reality of life in the Championship League, a significant step down from the Premier League that brings both practical challenges (lower revenue, reduced prestige) and psychological ones (wounded pride, uncertain future). This context makes Ted's philosophy particularly relevant, as it would be natural for the team to either panic about their reduced circumstances or fall into complacency about the supposedly "easier" competition.

Ted's wisdom comes at a moment when leadership clarity is essential. The team needs guidance on how to approach their new situation without being paralyzed by anxiety about what they've lost or becoming lazy about what they need to accomplish. His metaphor provides a framework for navigating this middle ground effectively. The quote also reflects Ted's personal approach to handling the various challenges he faces throughout Season 2, including his ongoing mental health struggles, his divorce proceedings, and the pressure to prove that the relegation was an aberration rather than a reflection of his coaching abilities. In each case, Ted tries to avoid both panic responses and avoidance behaviors, instead choosing measured, thoughtful action.

Understanding the Panic Button Response

The "panic button" represents our tendency to react to challenges with frantic, often counterproductive urgency. When we hit the panic button, we typically make decisions based on fear rather than wisdom, act hastily without proper consideration of consequences, and often create additional problems while trying to solve original ones. Panic responses are characterized by catastrophic thinking ("This is a disaster"), tunnel vision (focusing only on immediate threats while missing broader context), and reactive rather than responsive behavior. While the fight-or-flight response serves important functions in genuine emergencies, most modern challenges require calm analysis and strategic thinking rather than immediate, intense action.

Ted recognizes that panic not only feels terrible but also impairs our ability to think clearly and act effectively. When leaders panic, they often communicate that anxiety to their teams, creating organizational stress that makes collective problem-solving more difficult. By avoiding the panic button, Ted maintains the kind of steady presence that allows for better decision-making and inspires confidence in others.

Understanding the Snooze Button Response

The "snooze button" represents our tendency to avoid dealing with challenges by procrastinating, minimizing their importance, or hoping they'll resolve themselves without our active engagement. While this response feels more comfortable than panic, it's often equally counterproductive because problems typically worsen when ignored and opportunities disappear when not pursued promptly. Snooze button responses include procrastination on important decisions, avoiding difficult conversations, staying in comfortable routines when change is needed, and maintaining false optimism that problems will solve themselves. While this approach reduces immediate anxiety, it often creates larger problems over time and eliminates our agency in shaping outcomes.

Ted understands that the snooze button is particularly tempting when facing unpleasant realities or difficult tasks. It's natural to want to delay dealing with relegation, mental health issues, or relationship problems. However, his philosophy suggests that engagement, even when uncomfortable, is usually more effective than avoidance.

The Middle Path: Present and Engaged Action
Ted's approach advocates for what might be called "calm urgency"—recognizing the importance of challenges without being overwhelmed by them, taking action without being frantic, and staying engaged without being anxious. This middle path requires both emotional regulation (managing panic) and disciplinary commitment (avoiding procrastination). This balanced approach involves several key elements: accurate assessment of situations without catastrophizing or minimizing, strategic planning that considers both immediate needs and long-term consequences, steady action that addresses problems without creating new ones, and maintaining perspective that keeps individual challenges in a broader context.

Ted models this approach throughout the series. When facing relegation, he neither panics about the team's reduced status nor pretends that being in the Championship League doesn't matter. Instead, he acknowledges the challenge while focusing on what the team can control: their effort, their relationships, and their commitment to improvement.

Applications Throughout Season 2 and Beyond
This philosophy becomes particularly relevant as Ted faces his mental health challenges throughout Season 2. When experiencing panic attacks, Ted could either spiral into anxiety about his condition (hitting the panic button) or ignore his symptoms and avoid seeking help (hitting the snooze button). Instead, he gradually learns to acknowledge his struggles while taking constructive action to address them, including working with Dr. Sharon Fieldstone.

The principle also applies to how various characters handle their personal and professional challenges. Roy's transition from player to coach, Jamie's return to Richmond, and Rebecca's romantic developments all require navigation between panic and snooze responses. The characters who grow most effectively are those who learn to stay present with their challenges while taking thoughtful action.

The Broader Application to Daily Life

Ted's metaphor extends beyond crisis management to everyday decision-making and life management. Most people regularly face the choice between panic responses (overreacting to daily stresses) and snooze responses (procrastinating on important tasks or avoiding difficult conversations).

The wisdom suggests developing what psychologists call "distress tolerance"—the ability to stay present with uncomfortable feelings without either being overwhelmed by them or avoiding them entirely. This skill is fundamental to effective living, whether dealing with work pressures, relationship challenges, health issues, or opportunities for personal growth.

Explanation

The human tendency to oscillate between extremes when facing challenges represents one of our most consistent and counterproductive behavioral patterns. Ted's metaphor of avoiding both panic and snooze buttons addresses this tendency by identifying two equally problematic responses to difficulty and implicitly advocating for a more effective middle path.

The panic button response emerges from our evolutionary fight-or-flight system, which served our ancestors well when facing immediate physical threats but often misfires in response to modern psychological challenges. When we perceive threats—whether to our security, relationships, reputation, or goals—our nervous system can trigger intense arousal that impairs higher-order thinking and leads to reactive rather than responsive behavior.

Research in neuroscience shows that high anxiety and panic states literally reduce activity in the prefrontal cortex, the brain region responsible for executive functions like planning, decision-making, and impulse control. This explains why people in panic often make decisions they later regret, act in ways that seem obviously counterproductive in retrospect, and struggle to consider long-term consequences of immediate actions.

Conversely, the snooze button response often stems from what psychologists call "avoidance coping", the tendency to manage distress by avoiding or delaying engagement with stressful situations. While this approach provides temporary relief from anxiety, research consistently shows that avoidance coping leads to worse long-term outcomes across virtually all domains of life, from health and relationships to work and personal growth. Avoidance behaviors often compound problems over time because issues that require attention tend to worsen when ignored, opportunities have expiration dates, and procrastination itself becomes a source of stress and self-criticism. Additionally, avoiding challenges prevents us from developing the confidence and skills that come from successfully navigating difficult situations.

The middle path between panic and snooze requires developing several key psychological skills. Emotional regulation allows us to stay calm enough to think clearly while remaining alert enough to take necessary action. Distress tolerance enables us to remain present with uncomfortable feelings without being overwhelmed or trying to escape them immediately. And cognitive flexibility helps us consider multiple options and adapt our approach as circumstances change.

This balanced approach also requires what might be called "temporal perspective"—the ability to consider both immediate needs and long-term consequences when making decisions. Panic responses often sacrifice long-term effectiveness for short-term anxiety relief, while snooze responses sacrifice long-term benefits for short-term comfort avoidance.

Application

Try this four-step practice to develop the ability to stay between panic and snooze when facing challenges:

1. **Recognize Your Default Patterns:** Pay attention to how you typically respond to stress, uncertainty, or challenges. Do you tend to hit the "panic button" by overreacting, making hasty

decisions, or catastrophizing about potential outcomes? Or do you tend to hit the "snooze button" by procrastinating, avoiding difficult conversations, or hoping problems will resolve themselves?

2. **Practice the Pause:** When facing a challenging situation, before taking any action, practice taking a deliberate pause to regulate your emotional state and assess the situation accurately.

3. **Engage in Strategic Assessment:** Once you've regulated your initial emotional response, assess the situation using questions like: "What exactly is the problem I need to address?" "What are my realistic options for responding?" "What are the likely short-term and long-term consequences of different approaches?" This assessment helps you choose proportionate responses rather than over- or under-reacting.

4. **Take Measured Action:** Based on your assessment, choose actions that address the challenge without being driven by panic or delayed by avoidance.

Remember that developing this balance between panic and snooze is an ongoing practice that improves with experience. Some situations will naturally trigger stronger emotional reactions than others, and it's normal to default to old patterns under stress occasionally. Also, understand that the "right" level of urgency varies depending on the situation. Some challenges do require quick action, while others benefit from more extended consideration. The key is choosing your response level consciously rather than automatically defaulting to panic or avoidance patterns.

Most importantly, extend patience to yourself as you develop these skills. Learning to stay present and engaged with challenges while maintaining emotional balance is one of the most valuable life skills you can develop, but it takes time and practice to master.

Takeaway

Every time you choose to stay present and engaged with challenges rather than panicking or avoiding them, you build resilience, develop problem-solving skills, and create better outcomes for yourself and others around you. You also model effective stress management that can inspire others to approach their own challenges more skillfully.

The most effective people aren't those who never face difficulties. They're those who have learned to navigate challenges with calm engagement, neither being overwhelmed by problems nor ignoring them until they become crises. They understand that both panic and procrastination typically make situations worse, while thoughtful, measured action usually makes them better.

The next time you face a challenging situation, remember Ted's wisdom and ask yourself: "Am I tempted to hit the panic button or the snooze button right now?" "What would calm, engaged action look like in this situation?" "How can I stay present with this challenge without being overwhelmed by it or avoiding it entirely?"

After all, as Ted demonstrates throughout Season 2 and beyond, life's challenges require us to be alert without being anxious, engaged without being frantic, and proactive without being reactive. The space between panic and snooze is where effective living happens.

There's wisdom in avoiding both buttons. Stay present, take action, and trust your ability to handle whatever comes your way.

Lesson #15:
Your Choices Define You More

The Example:

Ted's quote: "*It is our choices, gentlemen, that show what we truly are, far more than our abilities.*"

--- Ted Lasso, Season 2, Episode 12: "Inverting the Pyramid of Success"

This profound observation occurs during the Season 2 finale, a pivotal episode that explores the aftermath of Nate's betrayal and the team's complex dynamics as they prepare for their final match. The timing is crucial. Ted delivers this wisdom at a moment when the characters are facing fundamental questions about identity, loyalty, and what it means to be a good person when talent and opportunity create competing pressures.

The quote itself is borrowed from Albus Dumbledore in Harry Potter, but Ted's use of it demonstrates his ability to find wisdom wherever it exists and apply it to the real-world challenges his team faces. This isn't just literary name-dropping; it's Ted recognizing that some truths transcend their original context and speak to universal human experiences.

Context
Here's the context:

- Ted delivers this wisdom during this season finale, which forces multiple characters to confront the gap between their abilities and their choices.

- The quote applies to various character arcs where talent remains constant, but choices determine outcomes.
- Jamie's redemption, Nate's betrayal, and Roy's growth all illustrate the principle that choices reveal character more than abilities.
- Ted models this philosophy through his own response to mental health challenges and personal betrayals.
- The series consistently shows that relationships, impact, and legacy are built through choices rather than natural gifts.
- The timing in the season 2 finale emphasizes that character development is the ultimate measure of success.

The Context of Season 2's Moral Complexity

By the season 2 finale, "Inverting the Pyramid of Success," multiple characters are grappling with choices that will define their character far more than their natural abilities ever could. Nate has revealed himself as the source of leaked information about Ted's panic attacks, Roy is navigating his transition from player to coach, Jamie is working to redeem himself after his arrogant past, and Ted himself is dealing with personal challenges that test his fundamental beliefs about leadership and forgiveness.

The episode title itself, "Inverting the Pyramid of Success," suggests that traditional metrics of achievement (wins, individual accolades, technical skills) are being turned upside down in favor of character-based measures of success. In this context, Ted's reminder about choices versus abilities becomes both a coaching philosophy and a moral framework.

Ted delivers this wisdom to his players at a time when they're facing not just athletic challenges but ethical ones. How do you respond when a teammate betrays the team? How do you handle success without losing your humility? How do you support each other when personal ambitions and team goals conflict? These questions can't be answered through talent alone. They require character, which is built through the accumulation of choices over time.

The Universal Truth About Character and Talent

Ted's observation touches on a fundamental truth that runs counter to much of our culture's emphasis on natural ability, inherited advantages, and innate talents. While abilities certainly matter and can open doors or create opportunities, they don't determine the kind of person you become or the impact you have on others. Those outcomes are determined by the choices you make, especially when those choices are difficult or when no one is watching.

This principle is particularly relevant in the high-pressure, high-talent world of professional sports, where extraordinary abilities can sometimes mask character deficiencies or where the temptation exists to believe that talent excuses poor choices. Ted's reminder helps his players understand that their legacy will be determined not by how well they can kick a football, but by how they choose to treat each other, handle adversity, and use their platform.

The timing of this quote in the season 2 finale makes it especially powerful because viewers have watched characters make crucial choices throughout the season. Jamie's decision to work on himself and return to Richmond, Roy's choice to embrace vulnerability and seek help, Rebecca's decision to be honest about her motivations, and yes, Nate's choice to betray Ted's confidence—all of these demonstrate how choices reveal character in ways that pure ability never could.

Examples Throughout the Series

The series consistently demonstrates this principle through character arcs that show people with similar abilities making vastly different choices and experiencing vastly different outcomes as a result. Jamie Tartt and Nate Shelley, for example, both possess exceptional football intelligence and talent, but their character trajectories diverge based on the choices they make when facing challenges to their ego and sense of importance.

Jamie's redemption arc shows someone choosing to prioritize team success over individual glory, vulnerability over defensive arrogance, and growth over stagnation. His abilities as a player remain relatively constant, but his choices transform him from a divisive prima donna into a valued teammate and leader.

Conversely, Nate's downfall illustrates what happens when someone with considerable tactical abilities makes choices based on insecurity, revenge, and the need for external validation. His football knowledge doesn't disappear, but his poor choices ultimately undermine his relationships and his effectiveness as a coach.

Roy Kent's journey provides another example of how choices matter more than abilities. As his physical abilities decline due to age, Roy faces a choice: he can become bitter about his limitations, or he can find new ways to contribute through leadership, mentorship, and emotional growth. His choice to embrace vulnerability and seek therapy shows character development that has nothing to do with his athletic gifts but everything to do with his moral courage.

Ted's Personal Application of This Philosophy
Ted himself embodies this principle throughout the series. His coaching abilities are limited—he admits to knowing little about soccer tactics and relies heavily on Coach Beard for technical expertise. What makes Ted effective isn't his strategic brilliance but his consistent choice to prioritize people over winning, compassion over judgment, and personal growth over maintaining a facade of perfection.

When Ted faces his own mental health challenges, the choices he makes, initially avoiding therapy, then gradually opening up to Dr. Sharon Fieldstone, define him far more than his natural charisma or coaching instincts. His willingness to model vulnerability and seek help demonstrates the kind of character that can't be taught in coaching clinics but must be chosen moment by moment.

Similarly, Ted's response to Nate's betrayal becomes a defining choice that reveals his character. Rather than retaliating or publicly shaming Nate, Ted chooses grace and understanding, recognizing that Nate's actions stem from pain and insecurity rather than malice. This choice, difficult and countercultural as it is, shows Ted's true character more clearly than any tactical victory ever could.

The Broader Implications for Personal Development

This philosophy has profound implications for how we think about personal development, success, and self-worth. In a culture obsessed with talent, natural gifts, and genetic advantages, Ted's reminder shifts focus to the one area where everyone has equal opportunity: the choice of how to respond to circumstances, how to treat others, and what values to prioritize. This is particularly liberating for people who may feel disadvantaged by their natural abilities or circumstances. While you can't change your innate talents, family background, or many external circumstances, you always have the power to choose your character. Every day presents opportunities to choose courage over comfort, kindness over indifference, growth over stagnation, and integrity over convenience.

The quote also serves as a humbling reminder for those who do possess exceptional natural abilities. Talent without character often leads to wasted potential, damaged relationships, and ultimately hollow achievements. The most respected and impactful people in any field are typically those who combine their abilities with consistently good choices about how to use those gifts.

Explanation

The distinction between what we can do and who we choose to be represents one of the most fundamental concepts in moral philosophy, psychology, and human development. Ted's observation, borrowed from the wisdom of literature but applied to real-world coaching, cuts through the noise of talent worship and genetic determinism to focus on the one area where every person has complete agency: the power of choice.

Our culture tends to be fascinated by natural ability, inherited advantages, and innate talents. We celebrate child prodigies, athletic phenoms, and individuals who seem to excel in their chosen fields effortlessly. While these abilities are certainly impressive and can create opportunities, they tell us very little about the kind of person someone will become or the impact they'll have on the world around them. The most important qualities that determine life satisfaction, relationship success, and positive impact—qualities such as integrity, kindness, resilience, courage, and wisdom—are not determined by a genetic lottery. They're developed through the accumulation of daily choices, often small and unnoticed, that gradually build the architecture of character over time.

This principle is particularly relevant in environments where talent is highly valued and rewarded, such as professional sports, entertainment, or academia. In these contexts, there's often an implicit assumption that exceptional ability somehow justifies or excuses character deficiencies. Ted's reminder serves as a necessary corrective: no amount of talent can compensate for consistently poor choices, and no lack of natural ability can excuse us from the responsibility to choose good character.

The psychological research on this topic supports Ted's insight. Studies on moral development show that ethical behavior is primarily learned and practiced rather than innate. Character strengths like honesty, compassion, and courage can be developed by anyone willing to make consistent choices that reinforce these qualities, regardless of their natural temperament or inherited traits. Furthermore, research on success and life satisfaction consistently shows that character-based qualities are better predictors of long-term fulfillment than raw talent or ability. People with strong character traits tend to build better relationships, recover more effectively from setbacks, and find more meaning in their work and lives, regardless of their natural gifts.

The quote also highlights the democratic nature of character development. While not everyone can become a world-class athlete, musician, or scholar, everyone can choose to become a person of good character. This levels the playing field in the most important game of all: the development of a life worth living and relationships worth having.

This philosophy doesn't diminish the importance of developing and using our abilities, talent is valuable and should be cultivated. Instead, it puts ability in proper perspective as a tool that can be used for good or ill, depending on the character of the person wielding it. A talented person with poor character may achieve short-term success but will likely struggle with relationships and long-term satisfaction. Conversely, someone with modest abilities but strong character often achieves impact and fulfillment far beyond what their raw talent would suggest.

Application

Try this four-step practice to ensure your choices align with the character you want to develop:

1. **Identify Your Character Goals:** Just as you might set goals for developing skills or abilities, consciously identify the character traits you want to strengthen. Having clear character goals helps you recognize choice points where you can practice these qualities.

2. **Recognize Daily Choice Points:** Throughout each day, notice moments where you can choose character over convenience, principle over expedience, or long-term integrity over short-term advantage. Most character development happens through these small, daily choices rather than dramatic moments.

3. **Practice Character-Based Decision Making:** When facing difficult decisions, ask yourself: "What would the person I want to become do in this situation?" rather than "What's the easiest or most advantageous choice?" Remember that every choice is an opportunity to either build or erode the person you're becoming.

4. **Evaluate Your Growth Based on Character, Not Just Achievements:** Regularly assess your development by looking at your choices and character growth, not just your accomplishments or skill improvements.

Remember that character development is a lifelong process that requires patience with yourself while maintaining commitment to growth. You won't make perfect choices consistently, but the goal is to make progressively better choices that align with the person you want to become. Also, understand that developing good character often requires making choices that seem disadvantageous in the short term but build trust, relationships, and self-respect over time. The person who consistently chooses integrity over expedience may sometimes face immediate costs but usually experiences long-term benefits in terms of reputation, relationships, and personal satisfaction.

Most importantly, recognize that your ability to make character-based choices is not dependent on your natural talents, background, or circumstances. Regardless of what abilities you were born with, you have the power to choose courage, kindness, honesty, and growth every single day. These choices, accumulated over time, will define you far more clearly than any talent or achievement ever could.

Takeaway

Every day presents you with countless opportunities to choose the kind of person you want to become, and these choices matter infinitely more than the natural abilities you were born with. While you can't control your inherited talents or many external circumstances, you have complete control over your character, which is built one choice at a time.

The next time you're facing a difficult decision or evaluating your own growth, remember Ted's wisdom and ask yourself: "What does this choice reveal about who I'm becoming?" "Am I prioritizing character development alongside skill development?" "What would I want to be remembered for, my abilities or my choices?"

After all, as Ted reminds us through both his words and his example throughout the series, abilities may open doors and create opportunities, but it's our choices that determine what we do once we walk through those doors. Your character is the only thing that's entirely within your control, and it's the most important thing you'll ever develop.

Your choices define you far more than your talents ever will. Choose wisely.

Lesson #16:
Stop the Self-Criticism Symphony

The Example:

> Ted's quote: "*You beating yourself up is like Woody Allen playing the clarinet. I don't want to hear it.*"
>
> --- Ted Lasso to Roy Kent, Season 1, Episode 9: "All Apologies"

This memorable line comes during a pivotal moment in Roy Kent's character arc, delivered with Ted's signature blend of humor and profound insight, like getting life advice from a therapist who moonlights as a stand-up comedian. The setting is significant and frankly hilarious: Roy is struggling with his declining performance on the field, facing the painful reality that his legendary career is coming to an end. Rather than accepting this transition gracefully (which, let's be honest, would be completely out of character for Roy Kent), he's engaged in brutal self-criticism, replaying his mistakes and berating himself for no longer being the player he once was.

Context
Ted Lasso says the quote to Roy Kent.
- Ted uses this line to discourage Roy from being self-critical about his declining performance as team captain.
- The reference to Woody Allen's clarinet playing humorously conveys that self-blame is as unappealing to hear as Allen's music, lightening the message about overcoming negative self-talk.

- This episode focuses on Roy facing the possibility of being benched for the good of the team, while Rebecca reveals some past misdeeds.
- Ted's coaching philosophy in this moment reflects a compassionate, comic approach to supporting team members through moments of self-doubt.
- The quote exemplifies the series' theme of using humor and empathy to address personal struggles and encourage growth.

Ted finds Roy literally sitting in a garbage can filled with ice water, a physical manifestation of the mental torture Roy is inflicting on himself that's so absurd it would be comedy gold if it weren't so heartbreaking. Roy looks like "a brunette Oscar the Grouch," as Ted observes, but this self-punishment isn't helping him perform better or feel better. It's just creating more suffering without any constructive benefit, like trying to fix a broken phone by throwing it against the wall repeatedly.

The Woody Allen clarinet reference is perfectly chosen and brutal in its accuracy: Allen famously plays clarinet as a hobby and regularly performs with a jazz band, despite being, by most accounts, not particularly skilled at the instrument (imagine the musical equivalent of watching someone parallel park very badly, but with enthusiasm). The comparison implies something that's technically happening but isn't enjoyable to experience and serves no real purpose for anyone involved, like a car alarm at 3 AM or someone explaining cryptocurrency at a dinner party.

The Context of Roy's Self-Torture

Roy Kent represents a particular type of high achiever who has built his identity around being excellent at something specific. In his case, he was a football legend who could intimidate opponents just by existing on the same pitch. Throughout his career, Roy has been defined by his exceptional football skills, his leadership on the field (primarily through strategic swearing), and his reputation as one of the best players of his generation. Now, as age catches up with him and his performance declines, Roy is facing an identity crisis that he's trying to solve through self-punishment, which is about as effective as trying to cure a headache by hitting yourself with a hammer.

This episode takes place during a crucial period where Roy's struggles are becoming increasingly visible, like watching a superhero slowly lose their powers, but with more British cursing. The media is commenting on his declining performance (because sports journalists are basically professional dream-crushers), his teammates are noticing his limitations, and Roy himself can feel the difference between his current abilities and his peak performance. Rather than processing this transition constructively—perhaps through therapy, meditation, or at least a good cry—Roy has turned his competitive drive inward, becoming his own harshest critic and personal torturer.

Ted's intervention comes at precisely the right moment, before Roy's self-criticism can spiral into something even more destructive, like living in that garbage can or developing a full-time career as his own worst enemy. Ted recognizes that Roy's self-punishment isn't motivated by a genuine desire to improve but is preventing the kind of clear thinking and self-compassion that would allow Roy to navigate this difficult transition more successfully, preferably without resembling a disgruntled Sesame Street character.

The Destructive Nature of Excessive Self-Criticism
Ted's comparison to Woody Allen's clarinet playing illuminates something crucial about destructive self-criticism: it's unpleasant for everyone involved. It serves no constructive purpose, like a fire alarm that goes off when you burn toast, technically doing its job but creating way more drama than necessary. Just as Allen's clarinet playing may be technically proficient but doesn't produce beautiful music (unless one has an unusual taste in jazz), Roy's self-criticism is technically a form of self-evaluation. Still, it doesn't lead to positive change or improvement.

Roy's ice bath self-punishment is a perfect metaphor for how self-criticism often works: it feels like we're taking action to address our problems, but we're actually just making ourselves suffer without addressing the underlying issues. The physical discomfort matches the psychological discomfort, but neither leads to constructive solutions. It's like trying to fix a leaky roof by standing in the rain and feeling bad about it.

Ted's Alternative Approach

Throughout the series, Ted consistently models a different approach to mistakes and limitations: acknowledgment without self-torture, like a civilized person who can admit they burned dinner without setting themselves on fire. When Ted makes errors, he typically follows a pattern of recognizing the mistake, extracting any useful learning, making appropriate corrections, and then moving forward without extended self-punishment or dramatic ice-bath performances.

This approach isn't about lowering standards or accepting mediocrity. Ted still wants to win games and help his players succeed. He just understands that self-criticism beyond a certain point becomes counterproductive, like continuing to knock on a door after you realize nobody's home. There's a difference between healthy self-evaluation ("That play didn't work, let me think about why") and the kind of mental self-abuse that Roy is engaging in ("I'm a washed-up has-been who should probably just disappear into the nearest garbage can").

Ted's humor in delivering this message is also significant and strategically brilliant. By using a funny comparison, he helps Roy step back from the intensity of his self-criticism and see it from a different perspective, like getting someone to laugh at a horror movie by pointing out how ridiculous the monster's costume looks. Sometimes we need an outside observer to point out that our internal dialogue has become absurdly harsh and unhelpful, like having a friend tell us we've been wearing our shirt inside-out all day.

The Broader Pattern in the Series

This scene with Roy represents a broader pattern in Ted Lasso where characters learn to distinguish between constructive self-reflection and destructive self-criticism, the difference between helpful personal feedback and running your own internal torture chamber. Throughout the series, we see various characters trapped in cycles of self-punishment that prevent growth rather than promoting it, like hamsters on wheels that are somehow going in reverse.

Jamie Tartt's journey involves learning to separate his self-worth from his performance and his father's approval, which is like learning to breathe underwater: difficult but ultimately life-saving. His transformation from self-absorbed pretty boy to genuine team player includes learning to be kind to himself when he makes mistakes, rather than hearing his father's cruel voice echoing in his head like the world's worst motivational speaker.

Rebecca's arc involves moving past the self-blame and shame stemming from her marriage and divorce and learning that her ex-husband's betrayal wasn't her fault. This revelation seems evident from the outside but can be impossibly hard to internalize when you're the one living it. Her journey toward self-compassion coincides with her becoming a better leader and person, proving that being nice to yourself isn't selfish; it's practical.

Even Ted himself must eventually confront his own patterns of self-criticism, particularly around his role as a father and his mental health challenges. His panic attacks and struggles with being away from his son, Henry, reveal that even the most optimistic person can have a harsh internal critic. It's just usually better disguised and more polite about its cruelty.

The show consistently demonstrates that while accountability and honest self-assessment are valuable, like having a good mirror that shows you when you need to fix your hair, the kind of brutal internal criticism that many characters inflict on themselves is both unnecessary and counterproductive, like having a mirror that tells you you're ugly every time you look into it.

Explanation

The distinction between constructive self-reflection and destructive self-criticism is one of the most important yet poorly understood aspects of personal development and high performance—like knowing the difference between helpful feedback and just being mean to yourself for sport. Many people, especially high achievers, believe that being hard on themselves is necessary for maintaining standards and driving improvement. This belief, while understandable, is both psychologically harmful and practically counterproductive, like trying to motivate a horse by beating it instead of offering carrots.

When we're in a state of self-attack, our minds become focused on defending against the perceived threat (which, ironically, is coming from inside the house) rather than on problem-solving or skill development. The result is often a downward spiral where poor performance leads to self-criticism, which leads to increased anxiety and impaired performance, which leads to more self-criticism. It's like being trapped in a washing machine of negativity.

Breaking free from destructive self-criticism requires developing what psychologists call "metacognitive awareness"—the ability to observe our own thought patterns and recognize when they've become unhelpful, like having a therapist living in your head but one who actually knows what they're doing. This is exactly what Ted provides for Roy: an outside perspective that helps Roy see his self-criticism as a choice rather than a necessary response to his situation, like pointing out that he doesn't actually have to live in that garbage can.

Application

Try this four-step practice to transform destructive self-criticism into constructive self-compassion (and possibly avoid any garbage-can incidents):

1. **Develop Self-Criticism Awareness:** Start paying attention to your internal dialogue, particularly during moments of stress, disappointment, or perceived failure, basically, become a detective investigating your own thoughts, but without the trench coat.

2. **Practice the Friend Test:** When you catch yourself in harsh self-criticism, pause and ask: "What would I say to a close friend who was dealing with this exact situation. Then deliberately offer yourself the same compassion, understanding, and practical support you would give to

someone you care about, complete with the patience and encouragement you'd naturally provide.

3. **Reframe Global Criticism into Specific Learning:** Transform broad, character-based self-attacks into specific, behavior-focused observations, essentially, turn your inner drama queen into a practical problem-solver.

4. **Create Self-Compassion Rituals:** Develop specific practices that help you respond to mistakes and setbacks with kindness rather than criticism. You could even develop a physical gesture that reminds you to be kind to yourself, though probably avoid Roy's ice-bath approach.

Remember that developing self-compassion is a skill that takes practice, especially if you've spent years engaging in harsh self-criticism. It's like learning a new language where the vocabulary consists entirely of being nice to yourself. Be patient with yourself as you learn new ways of responding to mistakes and setbacks, and notice if you start criticizing yourself for not being better at self-compassion (which would be ironic but also completely normal). Also, understand that self-compassion doesn't mean eliminating all standards or avoiding accountability. It's not about becoming complacent or pretending everything is fine when it's not. The goal is to create an internal environment that supports learning, growth, and sustained high performance rather than one that undermines these outcomes through excessive harshness, like having a greenhouse for personal development instead of a torture chamber.

Most importantly, extend this practice to how you respond to others' mistakes and struggles. When you model self-compassion and respond to others with kindness during difficult moments, you help create environments where people can acknowledge problems honestly, learn from setbacks, and maintain the resilience necessary for continued growth and improvement. Basically, you become the kind of person others want to be around, especially when things get tough.

Takeaway

Every time you choose to respond to your mistakes and limitations with self-compassion rather than self-criticism, you create conditions that actually support improvement and learning, like providing fertile soil instead of rocky ground for your personal growth. You also model for others what it looks like to maintain high standards while treating yourself with basic human kindness, which is rarer than it should be but infinitely more effective than the alternative.

The most successful and resilient people aren't those who never make mistakes or face setbacks (those people probably don't exist, despite what social media suggests). They're those who have learned to respond to difficulties in ways that support recovery and growth rather than creating additional suffering. They understand that being your own worst enemy is neither necessary nor effective for achieving excellence, like having a personal trainer who just insults you instead of actually helping you get stronger.

After all, as Ted demonstrates throughout the series, you can hold yourself accountable without holding yourself hostage to harsh internal criticism. The goal is to become your own best supporter and most constructive critic, not your own worst enemy, think helpful coach, not abusive dictator. High standards and self-kindness aren't mutually exclusive; they're actually better together, like tea and biscuits or Roy Kent and creative swearing.

Beating yourself up may be happening, but just like Woody Allen's clarinet playing, nobody needs to hear it, especially you.

Lesson #17:
It's the Lack of Hope That Gets You

The Example:

> Ted's quote: "*So I've been hearing this phrase y'all got over here that I ain't too crazy about. 'It's the hope that kills you.' Y'all know that? I disagree, you know? I think it's the lack of hope that comes and gets you.*"
>
> --- Ted Lasso (Season 1, Episode 10: "The Hope That Kills You")

In the Season 1 finale of Ted Lasso, as AFC Richmond faces potential relegation and the weight of a disappointing season that's been about as successful as a chocolate teapot, Ted addresses one of the most cynical sayings in football culture, and perhaps in life itself. The phrase "It's the hope that kills you" has become a defensive mantra for fans who've been disappointed too many times, like a psychological security blanket made of pessimism and protective cynicism. It's a way of protecting themselves from the pain of expecting good things that don't come to pass, sort of like never ordering dessert so you can't be disappointed when it's sold out.

Context
To better understand this quote and its importance, here is some context:

- Season 1 finale with Richmond facing potential relegation from the Premier League.

- The final match of the season determines if they stay in the Premier League or get relegated.
- Facing criticism from the media and fans about his coaching methods.
- The phrase "it's the hope that kills you" is commonly used by British football fans about getting excited, only to be disappointed.
- British football culture often embraces protective pessimism
- Long-suffering fans use cynicism to shield themselves from repeated disappointments.
- The phrase reflects generations of fans whose teams have let them down.
- Ted delivers this speech before the crucial final match.
- He's addressing both his team and the broader philosophy of how to approach uncertainty.
- The speech comes when everything looks darkest, and most people expect failure.
- Ted is essentially arguing against the defensive pessimism that surrounds him.
- Richmond does get relegated despite Ted's optimism.
- However, the team and community are more united than before.
- The speech sets up Ted's philosophy that will carry through the remaining seasons.

But Ted, in his characteristic way of challenging conventional wisdom through simple truth-telling (and probably some folksy Kansas metaphors), offers an entirely different perspective that's about as welcome to British cynics as pineapple on pizza. He doesn't just disagree with the saying; he turns it on its head entirely, like a philosophical pancake flip. For Ted, hope isn't the problem; hopelessness is. Hope isn't what destroys us; the absence of hope is what truly damages our spirits, our relationships, and our ability to keep moving forward, like trying to drive a car with an empty gas tank and wondering why you're not getting anywhere.

This moment is compelling because Ted delivers it not from a place of naive optimism, the kind that believes everything will work out because you really, really want it to, but from someone who has experienced real disappointment and loss. By this point in the series, we know Ted is going through a divorce that's messier than a toddler eating spaghetti, struggling with panic attacks that hit him like surprise pop quizzes from his own anxiety, and facing the very real possibility that his team will be relegated despite his best efforts. He's not speaking from inexperience with pain; he's speaking from the hard-won wisdom of someone who has learned that hope is what sustains us through pain, not what causes it, like discovering that the life preserver, not the ocean, is what keeps you afloat.

Ted's reframing is revolutionary because it challenges a fundamental assumption about self-protection that's been around longer than bad British weather. The conventional wisdom suggests that if we don't hope for good things, we won't be disappointed when they don't happen. It's emotional hedging, like betting against your own happiness. But Ted recognizes that this approach doesn't actually protect us from pain; it just guarantees that we'll experience a different kind of suffering: the slow death of dreams deferred and possibilities unexplored, like voluntarily living in black and white when the world is actually in color.

What makes this philosophy so compelling is that Ted isn't advocating for blind optimism or unrealistic expectations; he's not suggesting that we all become delusional cheerleaders for the impossible. He's advocating for the courage to remain open to possibility even in the face of uncertainty, which is about as easy as it sounds and twice as scary. He understands that hope doesn't promise that good things will happen (that would be a warranty, not hope); it promises that good things are possible, and that possibility alone is worth maintaining even when outcomes are beyond our control, like planting seeds without knowing if it will rain.

The timing of this declaration is crucial and demonstrates Ted's remarkable emotional intelligence. Ted shares this wisdom not when everything is going well, when hope is easy and costs nothing, but when things look their darkest, like delivering a motivational speech during a thunderstorm. Richmond is likely to be relegated, his personal life is in turmoil, and many people are questioning his methods and his competence with the enthusiasm of armchair quarterbacks. It would be the perfect time to give in to cynicism or to protect himself through lowered expectations, like everyone else seems to be doing. Instead, he doubles down on hope as a conscious choice and a form of courage, the kind that requires no cape but plenty of heart.

The Context of British Football Fatalism

To fully appreciate Ted's radical hope philosophy, it's essential to understand the cultural context against which he's working. British football culture, particularly around clubs like Richmond that have seen more disappointments than a dating app, has developed a sophisticated system of protective pessimism. It's a culture where "cautious optimism" is considered dangerously reckless and "blind faith" is what you call someone who thinks their team might actually win something.

The phrase "It's the hope that kills you" isn't just a saying. It's practically a religious doctrine among long-suffering football fans. It's been passed down through generations like a family heirloom nobody actually wants but everyone feels obligated to keep. These fans have learned through painful experience that getting excited about their team's prospects is like touching a hot stove repeatedly and expecting different results.

Ted, coming from American sports culture where optimism is practically mandatory and "rebuilding year" is considered temporary rather than a permanent lifestyle, finds this defensive pessimism both fascinating and heartbreaking. In Kansas, hope isn't something you ration carefully; it's something you hand out like free samples at a grocery store. The cultural clash is like watching someone from a desert try to understand why people from a rainforest carry umbrellas everywhere.

The Science of Hope vs. Hopelessness

What Ted intuitively understands, and what psychology research consistently confirms, is that hope, and hopelessness aren't just opposite emotional states. They're different operating systems for human beings, like running on optimism software versus pessimism malware. Hope doesn't just make us feel better; it literally changes how our brains process information, solve problems, and respond to challenges.

When we maintain hope, even in difficult circumstances, our brains stay in what researchers call "approach mode." We continue looking for solutions, noticing opportunities, and investing energy in positive possibilities. We're like explorers who believe there might be treasure ahead, so we continue to map new territory. Hopelessness, on the other hand, triggers "avoidance mode," where our brains become primarily focused on preventing additional pain rather than creating positive outcomes. We become like people who've decided all maps are lies, so we stop exploring entirely.

Ted's observation that "it's the lack of hope that comes and gets you" is particularly astute because hopelessness isn't just the absence of something good. It's the presence of something actively harmful. Hopelessness doesn't just leave us neutral; it actively undermines our resilience, creativity, and ability to recognize opportunities when they appear. It's like having a really pessimistic roommate living in your head, constantly pointing out everything that could go wrong and nothing that could go right.

Examples from the Series

Throughout Ted Lasso, we see this hope philosophy play out in various character arcs. Rebecca's journey from bitter revenge plot to genuine team support perfectly illustrates Ted's point. When she's trapped in hopelessness about love and trust (thanks to Rupert's betrayal, which was worse than finding out your favorite restaurant has closed), she becomes actively destructive, hiring Ted specifically hoping he'll fail. But as Ted's relentless hope gradually infects her worldview like a benevolent virus, she transforms from saboteur to supporter, proving that hope really is contagious in the best possible way.

Jamie Tartt's evolution from selfish prima donna to team player also demonstrates the power of hope over hopelessness. When Jamie believes he's fundamentally unlovable (thanks to his father, who makes Darth Vader look like a caring parent), he becomes defensive, arrogant, and isolated. But as he begins to hope that he might be worthy of genuine friendship and respect, largely thanks to Ted's unwavering belief in his potential, he becomes the kind of teammate who brings birthday cakes and actually passes the ball to other people.

Even Roy Kent's retirement crisis illustrates this principle. When Roy loses hope about his playing career, he becomes a miserable ice-bath-dwelling grouch who's about as pleasant as a hangover on Christmas morning. But when he starts hoping for a different kind of future, first as a coach, then as a commentator, then as a full human being capable of growth, he transforms from angry has-been to someone who can actually smile without looking like he's in physical pain.

The series consistently shows that hope isn't just feel-good fluff. It's practical fuel for personal transformation. Characters who maintain hope, even when circumstances are objectively terrible, find ways to grow and improve. Characters who abandon hope, even when their circumstances aren't that bad, tend to stagnate or actively make things worse for themselves and everyone around them.

Explanation

Ted's philosophy about hope versus hopelessness touches on one of the fundamental choices we face in life: how to respond to uncertainty and the possibility of disappointment, basically, how to live in a world where good things aren't guaranteed but bad things aren't either. The saying "It's the hope that kills you" reflects a common strategy for managing emotional risk that's about as effective as wearing a raincoat in a swimming pool. The logic goes: if we don't expect good things, we can't be hurt when they don't materialize. It's emotional insurance with a really high deductible.

But Ted's counter-argument reveals the hidden costs of this protective strategy, like discovering that your insurance policy actually makes you more likely to get in accidents. When we abandon hope to avoid disappointment, we don't actually eliminate suffering; we just trade the sharp pain of occasional disappointment for the chronic ache of living without possibility. Hopelessness doesn't protect us from hurt—it guarantees a different kind of hurt, one that slowly erodes our capacity for joy, connection, and growth, like emotional rust that spreads until everything becomes dull and lifeless.

The power of hope lies not in its ability to control outcomes (hope is not a remote control for the universe), but in its ability to sustain us through the process of working toward those outcomes. When we maintain hope, we continue to put effort into our goals, to invest in relationships, to take risks that might lead to growth or positive change. We're like gardeners who keep planting seeds even when the weather's been bad, because we know that eventually conditions might improve, and we want to be ready when they do. Without hope, we tend to withdraw our energy and engagement, creating a self-fulfilling prophecy that's more predictable than a British weather report: our lack of expectation leads to lack of effort, which leads to poor outcomes, which reinforces our hopelessness, which leads to even less effort. It's like a really depressing version of compound interest, where negativity builds on itself until you're earning a steady return on your investment in misery.

Ted's insight also recognizes that hope is fundamentally about agency and possibility. It's about believing that our actions might matter and that circumstances might change. When we believe that good things might happen, we're more likely to position ourselves to recognize and seize opportunities when they arise, like having our antennae up for positive possibilities. We stay alert to chances that hopeless people might miss entirely, continue to build relationships that might prove valuable, develop skills that might come in handy, and maintain the energy needed to respond positively when circumstances improve.

Furthermore, hope has a social dimension that cynicism lacks, like the difference between being the person everyone wants at their party versus the person everyone hopes won't show up. Hopeful people tend to be more pleasant to be around (shocking, we know), more supportive of others' dreams, and more likely to contribute positively to their communities. Hope is contagious in the best possible way—it creates environments where others feel permission to hope as well, leading to collective efforts that can actually improve outcomes for everyone involved, like a positive feedback loop that actually feeds back something useful.

Application

Implementing Ted's hope philosophy requires both intellectual understanding and practical strategies for maintaining optimism in the face of uncertainty. You need both the theory and the practice, like learning to drive by reading the manual and actually getting behind the wheel. Here's how to cultivate this approach without turning into an insufferable optimist who thinks everything happens for a reason:

1. **Distinguish Hope from Expectation:** Practice separating your hope for positive outcomes from your expectation that they will occur. Hope says, "This good thing is possible and worth working toward," like planting a garden because vegetables might grow. Expectation suggests that "this good thing will definitely happen," much like demanding that your garden produce prize-winning tomatoes, regardless of the weather, soil, or your actual gardening skills.

2. **Identify Your Hope-Killing Thoughts:** Pay attention to the mental patterns that drain your sense of possibility faster than a phone battery on 1%. When you notice these patterns, consciously challenge them with more hopeful but realistic alternatives, like having a debate with your inner pessimist, but actually winning for once.

3. **Build Hope Through Small Successes:** When facing large challenges that might overwhelm your sense of possibility, break them down into smaller goals where success is more achievable. Each small success builds your capacity to hope for larger ones, creating positive momentum that sustains optimism through longer-term challenges.

4. **Reframe Disappointments as Information:** When hopes don't materialize as expected, practice viewing disappointments as information rather than evidence that hope is foolish. This approach helps you maintain your capacity for future hope while learning from experience, like treating setbacks as course corrections rather than proof that the destination doesn't exist.

Takeaway

Ted Lasso's challenge to the cynical wisdom of "It's the hope that kills you" offers us a profound reframe about one of life's most fundamental choices, and it's a choice we make every day, sometimes every hour. His insight that "it's the lack of hope that comes and gets you" reveals that our attempts to protect ourselves from disappointment often cause more suffering than the disappointments themselves would, like wearing a helmet everywhere to avoid head injuries but never actually going outside to live life.

This doesn't mean that hope is always easy or that maintaining optimism doesn't require courage; it definitely does, because hope makes us vulnerable in a world that doesn't come with guarantees. Ted's philosophy acknowledges that hoping does make us vulnerable to disappointment, but it argues that this vulnerability is preferable to the guaranteed diminishment that comes with hopelessness. When we abandon hope, we don't just protect ourselves from potential future pain; we rob ourselves of present joy, future possibility, and the energy needed to create positive change, like voluntarily moving to a smaller, darker apartment to avoid the risk of ever having to move again.

The beauty of Ted's approach is that it's grounded in experience rather than naivety. He's not a sheltered optimist who has never faced real challenges. He's someone who has learned that disappointment is survivable, but hopelessness is soul-destroying, like discovering that temporary pain is preferable to permanent numbness. He understands that we can endure the sharp sting of specific hopes not materializing, but we struggle to thrive when we lose our fundamental belief in the possibility of good things happening.

Perhaps most importantly, Ted's insight reminds us that hope is a choice we make daily, sometimes moment by moment, like deciding what channel to watch but for our entire worldview. We can't control outcomes, but we can control our orientation toward possibility. We can't guarantee that our hopes will be fulfilled, but we can guarantee that abandoning hope will limit our ability to recognize and create opportunities for positive change when they arise.

Ultimately, Ted's philosophy suggests that hope is not merely an emotional stance, but a practical strategy for navigating an uncertain world that's more effective than its alternatives. It keeps us engaged, alert to opportunities, and connected to others in ways that actually increase the likelihood of positive outcomes. While hope doesn't guarantee that good things will happen, hopelessness almost guarantees that we won't be positioned to recognize or create good things when they become possible.

The choice between hope and hopelessness isn't about avoiding pain; both paths involve some suffering. It's about choosing which kind of life we want to live and which type of person we want to be.

Lesson #18:
Total Football is Life

The Example:

> Coach Beard's quote: "*Total Football is about letting go of your baggage and trusting your intuition. It's jazz. It's Motown. It's Mamet. It's Pinter. It's Einstein. It's Keurig. It's Gaga. ... It's about throwing off the constraints put upon you by society and by yourselves. We all know football is life. But a beautiful life is Total Football.*"
>
> --- Coach Beard (Season 2, Episode 8: "Man City")

In one of the Ted Lasso show's most philosophically rich moments, the kind that makes you wonder if Beard has been secretly auditing philosophy courses online, Coach Beard delivers this poetic meditation on Total Football that transcends sports strategy and becomes a manifesto for living authentically. The scene occurs during a crucial match against Manchester City, where Richmond faces a team that plays with the fluidity and interconnectedness that defines Total Football.

Context

Here's the context for Coach Beard's Total Football quote from Richmond is playing Manchester City in a crucial FA Cup semifinal match:

- Man City is demonstrating superior tactical play with fluid, interconnected football, while Richmond is struggling to match City's seamless style of play.

- Their style contrasts sharply with Richmond's more rigid tactical approach.
- Beard recognizes they're witnessing something beyond just football tactics.
- His analysis transcends sports and becomes a life philosophy.
- The quote links football strategy to life philosophy about being true to yourself.

As Beard watches the opposing team's seamless, almost telepathic play, he doesn't just see a tactical system. He sees a metaphor for life itself, because apparently, everything reminds Beard of something profound. His eclectic references span jazz improvisation, Motown's soulful collaboration, the rhythmic precision of David Mamet's dialogue, the pregnant pauses of Harold Pinter's theater, Einstein's revolutionary thinking, the simple efficiency of a Keurig coffee maker, and Lady Gaga's fearless self-expression.

What makes this moment so powerful is how Beard recognizes that Total Football isn't really about football at all. It's about the courage to be fully yourself while remaining beautifully connected to others, like being part of a jazz ensemble where everyone gets to solo. Still, nobody forgets they're making music together. It's about trusting your instincts when the playbook fails, flowing between different versions of yourself as circumstances demand, and playing your position while staying open to playing others when the moment calls for it, basically, being a Swiss Army knife in human form.

In traditional football, players are locked into specific roles with the rigidity of a British queue: defenders defend, midfielders control the middle, strikers score, and everyone stays in their lane like good little tactical soldiers. But Total Football asks the revolutionary question: what if everyone could do everything? What if the boundaries were fluid? What if the beauty came not from perfection within constraints, but from the elegant dance of adaptation and trust? It's like asking what would happen if everyone at a dinner party could cook, serve, entertain, and clean up, all while seamlessly switching roles based on what's needed most in the moment.

Beard sees this philosophy everywhere, in Miles Davis trusting his trumpet to find the right note without sheet music, in the Temptations seamlessly blending individual voices into harmonic perfection, in Einstein abandoning classical physics to discover relativity, in Gaga refusing to fit into pop music's prescribed boxes. Each represents the same revolutionary act: letting go of what you're "supposed" to be and trusting what you actually are, which is scarier than it sounds but infinitely more rewarding.

The scene serves as a masterclass in seeing connections across disciplines and recognizing universal principles that apply far beyond their original context. Beard doesn't just coach football; he coaches life, using the pitch as a laboratory for exploring what it means to be fully human, as if Socrates had really good tactical awareness and an inexplicably extensive knowledge of pop culture references.

The Context of Beard's Brilliance

To fully appreciate this moment, it's worth noting that this is the same Coach Beard who once spent an entire episode wandering London after a devastating loss, ending up in underground clubs and having philosophical conversations with strangers, basically, the man processes football defeats like they're existential crises, which makes perfect sense when you think about it. Throughout the series, Beard has been the quiet intellectual counterpart to Ted's folksy wisdom, the kind of person who probably reads Nietzsche for fun and somehow makes it relevant to corner kick strategies.

This Total Football speech comes after Richmond has been getting thoroughly outplayed by Manchester City, a team that embodies everything Beard is describing. They move like water, anticipate each other's thoughts, and make the beautiful game look genuinely beautiful rather than just a bunch of people chasing a ball around a field. It's the kind of performance that makes you understand why people call football "the beautiful game" instead of "the kicking sport" or "organized running with occasional scoring."

Beard's philosophical approach to football analysis is quintessentially him. Where Ted might offer a homespun metaphor about Kansas weather patterns, Beard drops references that span centuries of human creativity and innovation. It's like having a Renaissance scholar explain why your team lost, but somehow making it inspiring instead of just intellectually intimidating.

The Genius of Eclectic References
Beard's seemingly random cultural references actually form a brilliant tapestry of human creativity and rule-breaking that makes perfect sense once you think about it. Jazz improvisation is perhaps the most obvious parallel. Musicians who know the rules so well they can break them beautifully, creating something new in the moment that somehow feels both spontaneous and inevitable. It's like watching Coltrane take a simple melody and transform it into something that didn't exist five minutes earlier but feels like it always should have.

Motown represents collaborative excellence, different voices and instruments coming together to create something larger than any individual contribution, like the Supremes or the Temptations, proving that synchronized creativity can be both disciplined and joyful. These weren't just singers standing next to each other; they were musical organisms that moved and sounded like unified entities while still showcasing individual brilliance.

Einstein's inclusion makes sense when you consider that relativity was essentially about throwing out the assumption that space and time are fixed and separate, much like Total Football throws out the assumption that player positions are fixed and separate. Sometimes the biggest breakthroughs come from questioning the most basic assumptions about how things are supposed to work.

The Keurig reference is actually brilliant in its mundanity. Here's a simple innovation that asked, "What if making coffee didn't require all this complicated equipment and timing?" and revolutionized morning routines worldwide. Sometimes Total Football thinking is about complex artistic expression, and sometimes it's about finding elegantly simple solutions to everyday problems.

Lady Gaga represents fearless self-expression and the refusal to be categorized. She's a pop star who's also a jazz artist, an actress, an activist, and occasionally someone who wears a dress made of raw meat to award shows because why not? She embodies the Total Football principle of refusing to stay in one lane when you have the talent and vision to excel in multiple areas.

Explanation

When Beard describes Total Football as "letting go of your baggage and trusting your intuition," he's identifying the two greatest obstacles to living authentically: the psychological stuff we carry around like overpacked suitcases, and the fear that keeps us from trusting our inner wisdom, basically, the difference between being weighed down by your past and being paralyzed by uncertainty about your future.

Baggage comes in many forms, and most of us are carrying around more than we realize, like emotional hoarders who've forgotten what we actually need versus what we're just hanging onto out of habit. Sometimes it's literal, the career path chosen to please parents who wanted you to be a doctor when you clearly should have been a chef, the relationship patterns learned from childhood that made sense when you were eight but are counterproductive now that you're thirty-eight, the limiting beliefs acquired through painful experiences that were accurate for that specific situation but have become universal life rules. Other times it's more subtle, the voice that says "people like me don't do that" (which usually means "people from my background/class/family don't take those kinds of risks"), the fear of judgment that keeps us playing small and safe, the perfectionism that prevents us from trying anything we might not immediately excel at because better not to try than to be publicly mediocre.

This baggage doesn't just weigh us down like carrying rocks in our backpack; it forces us into rigid positions, like traditional football players locked into predetermined roles that made sense when the game was simpler but might not serve the current situation. We become "the responsible one," "the creative one," "the analytical one," or "the people-pleaser," and we defend these positions fiercely because they feel safe and familiar, like wearing the same outfit every day, because at least you know it fits and matches. But Total Football, and a beautiful life, asks us to consider: what if you could be all of these things? What if your identity could be as fluid and adaptive as the situation demands, like being a different person at brunch than you are in a board meeting, not because you're fake, but because you contain multitudes?

The beautiful paradox of Total Football is that this individual freedom creates better collective outcomes. When each player trusts themselves enough to move fluidly, the entire team becomes more responsive, more creative, and more alive, much like a jazz ensemble where everyone's individual excellence contributes to something none of them could create alone. Similarly, when we show up authentically in our relationships and work, we don't just serve ourselves. We give others permission to do the same, creating environments where everyone can play to their full potential instead of just the roles they've been assigned or have assigned themselves.

Ted himself embodies Total Football coaching. He refuses to stay locked into the traditional role of "tactical mastermind" and instead flows between being a therapist, a teacher, a friend, a philosopher, and yes, occasionally even a football coach. His willingness to play multiple roles based on what his players need in the moment makes him more effective than coaches who stick rigidly to one approach.

Application

Implementing Total Football thinking in your life requires both strategic awareness and tactical flexibility. Basically, you need to know what positions you're capable of playing and be willing to switch between them as circumstances demand. Here's how to begin your own personal Total Football revolution:

1. **Identify Your Current Position:** Take inventory of the roles you play—at work, in relationships, in your community, even in your own head. Notice which ones feel natural and energizing (like playing your preferred position), and which feel like constraints or costumes you put on because they're

expected (like being forced to play goalkeeper when you're clearly a striker at heart).

2. **Examine Your Baggage:** What beliefs about yourself or your capabilities are you carrying that no longer serve you, like outdated software that's slowing down your entire system? Often, what we think are immutable facts about ourselves are just outdated strategies for navigating situations that no longer exist.

3. **Practice Small Pivots:** Start with low-stakes situations where you can experiment with fluid thinking. In meetings, instead of defaulting to your usual role, ask: "What would serve this situation best right now?" Maybe the detail-oriented person offers a big-picture perspective, or the quiet observer shares a bold idea, or the normally supportive person pushes back on something that doesn't make sense.

4. **Build Your Improvisation Skills:** Like jazz musicians who practice scales so they can improvise freely, develop competencies outside your comfort zone so you have more positions you can play when life demands flexibility.

Remember, the goal isn't to abandon all structure. Even Total Football has principles and patterns, rules and boundaries that make creativity possible. The goal is to hold structure lightly enough that you can adapt when the situation calls for something different, like being a master chef who knows the fundamentals so well that they can improvise when they discover the salmon is overcooked but the vegetables are perfect.

Takeaway

Total Football reveals a profound truth that applies far beyond sports: the most beautiful performances, whether on a pitch, in a boardroom, in a relationship, or in life, happen when people are free to be fully themselves while remaining deeply connected to the whole. It's not chaos masquerading as strategy; it's organized freedom. It's not selfish individualism disguised as teamwork; it's enlightened collaboration where everyone's authenticity contributes to collective success.

When you let go of the baggage that keeps you playing the same position over and over (like being stuck on repeat in a role that stopped fitting years ago), and when you trust your intuition to guide you into new spaces, you don't just change your own game. You make it possible for everyone around you to play more freely as well. You become part of something larger and more beautiful than any individual performance could achieve, like joining an orchestra where everyone's unique instrument contributes to a symphony that none of them could create alone.

The constraints that society and your own fears have placed on you aren't immutable laws of physics—they're just one way the game has been played, like following a recipe when you could be creating your own dish. Total Football asks: what if there's a more beautiful way? What if the very thing you think disqualifies you—your unconventional background, your different perspective, your refusal to fit neatly into categories—is actually your greatest strength, like being a secret weapon disguised as a liability?

As Coach Beard reminds us in one of his moments of philosophical brilliance, we all know that football is life. But a beautiful life, one lived with courage, creativity, and connection, is Total Football. It's about playing every position your heart calls you to play, trusting your teammates to do the same, and creating something together that none of you could create alone, like being part of a jazz ensemble, a Motown group, a revolutionary scientific discovery, a perfectly simple coffee-making innovation, and a fearlessly creative pop performance all at the same time.

The beautiful game isn't just happening on the pitch. It's happening everywhere: people choose to let go of their baggage, trust their intuition, and play with the fluid grace of those who know that the most important position is simply being authentically and courageously themselves.

Lesson #19:
The Isaac Cut—Small Acts, Big Love

The Example:

> The Isaac Cut: A symbolic gesture of acceptance and solidarity (also known as "the most emotionally devastating haircut in television history").
>
> --- Isaac McAdoo's action (Season 3, Episode 9: "La Locker Room Aux Folles")

In one of the Ted Lasso show's most quietly powerful moments, Team captain Isaac McAdoo picks up a pair of scissors and offers to cut Colin Hughes's hair. On the surface, it's a simple gesture. Still, in the context of Colin's recent coming out to the team, this moment becomes something much more profound: a wordless declaration of acceptance, support, and unconditional love that resonates more deeply than any touchdown celebration or victory speech ever could.

Context

To appreciate the gesture, you need to understand the background and context.

- Colin has been struggling with his identity as a closeted gay man throughout the series.
- Previous episodes showed him navigating carefully around teammates and avoiding personal conversations.
- The locker room has traditionally been a space he felt he had to be guarded in.
- Colin finds himself in the locker room with his teammates

- Colin shares that he's gay with visible nervousness and vulnerability.
- The locker room falls completely silent as teammates process this revelation.
- The tension is palpable as Colin waits for their reaction
- Isaac, as team captain, recognizes this as a leadership moment.
- Instead of making speeches or grand gestures, he picks up scissors, and he offers to cut Colin's hair, a practical, intimate gesture.
- His action immediately breaks the tension and sets the tone for acceptance.
- The locker room becomes a sanctuary instead of a place of fear.

Isaac's response is perfect in its simplicity. He doesn't make speeches about tolerance or inclusion. He doesn't awkwardly stumble over words trying to express support. Instead, he does something beautifully ordinary: he offers to help Colin with something practical and personal, like the world's most mundane yet meaningful task. The act of cutting someone's hair requires trust, intimacy, and care. It's not something you do for someone you merely tolerate or someone you're trying to keep at arm's length. It's a service that says, "I see you, I accept you, and I'm here for you."

What makes the Isaac Cut so powerful is that it transforms what could have been an awkward or emotionally charged moment into something tender and normal, like turning a potential therapy session into a casual chat between friends. By offering this simple service, Isaac is essentially saying, "You're still you. You're still our teammate. Nothing has changed about how we care for each other," which is exactly what Colin needed to hear without actually having to hear it spelled out in words.

The scene also reveals Isaac's evolution as a leader, from someone who once seemed more interested in looking cool than actually leading to someone who understands that true leadership sometimes involves picking up scissors and making someone feel less alone. Earlier in the series, we've seen him struggle with his own vulnerabilities and insecurities about captaining the team. Remember when he couldn't even speak during that team meeting and just made intimidating faces instead? But here, in this crucial moment, he steps into true leadership not by giving orders or making demands (his usual approach), but by offering presence, acceptance, and practical love. He creates space for vulnerability by responding to it with simple, genuine care, like being a human security blanket, but more useful.

The Context of Colin's Journey
To fully appreciate the Isaac Cut, it's worth remembering Colin's journey throughout the series. He's been the quiet one, the background player who does his job without much fanfare, basically, the human equivalent of a reliable car that never breaks down but doesn't win any beauty contests either. We've seen glimpses of his personal struggles, his careful navigation of a world where being different feels dangerous, and his gradual building of trust with his teammates.

Colin's coming-out scene is preceded by moments where we see him struggle with his identity while watching his teammates become more open and genuine with each other. There's something beautifully symbolic about him choosing to come out in the locker room. It's the very space that symbolizes traditional masculinity and could have been his most significant source of fear, but it becomes the place where he finds his greatest acceptance.

The episode title "La Locker Room Aux Folles" is itself a playful reference to the musical "La Cage aux Folles," which deals with themes of acceptance and found family, basically, the show's writers being as subtle as a neon sign, but in the best possible way. The Richmond locker room becomes its own kind of stage where real-life drama unfolds with more authenticity than most theatrical productions.

Isaac's response is even more meaningful when you consider his own character development. Remember early Isaac, who was all scowls and intimidation, who seemed to think leadership meant being the scariest person in the room? His transformation into someone who responds to vulnerability with tenderness shows how much he's internalized Ted's lessons about what real strength looks like.

The Anatomy of Small Gestures

Think about the alternatives Isaac could have chosen. He could have given a speech about acceptance (awkward and potentially preachy). He could have organized some team meeting about diversity and inclusion (well-intentioned but treating Colin like a learning opportunity rather than a person). He could have made a big public statement of support (putting Colin in the spotlight when he probably just wanted to be treated normally). Instead, he offers to cut Colin's hair, which is simultaneously the most ordinary and most extraordinary thing he could do.

The genius of this gesture is in its ordinariness. It's the kind of thing teammates do for each other all the time, except this time it carries the weight of acceptance and belonging. It's like code-switching from "this is a Big Moment" to "this is just Tuesday," which allows Colin to experience acceptance without feeling like he's become the team's diversity project or inspirational poster child.

Throughout the series, we see other examples of small gestures that carry enormous weight. Ted bringing Rebecca biscuits isn't just about snacks; it's about consistency, care, and the kind of daily kindness that builds trust over time. Roy teaching Phoebe to curse properly isn't just about vocabulary; it's about treating her as a full person worthy of honest communication. These small acts accumulate into something much larger than their individual components, like compound interest but for human connection.

Explanation

The Isaac Cut represents the profound impact of small, intentional acts of love and acceptance. This kind doesn't make headlines but changes lives, like the difference between a greeting card sentiment and an actual hug from someone who cares about you. In moments when people are most vulnerable, when they're sharing their truth, facing a crisis, or needing support, grand gestures often feel hollow or performative, like receiving a gift that's obviously more about the giver feeling good than about meeting your actual needs. What matters most are the small, genuine acts that communicate presence, care, and acceptance without requiring a parade or a press release.

This concept challenges our cultural tendency to believe that meaningful support requires big, dramatic actions, probably because we've been conditioned by movies where love is proven through elaborate schemes and problems are solved through passionate speeches. We often think we need to have perfect words (which don't exist), organize major interventions (which are exhausting), or make sweeping changes (which are often impractical) to help someone truly. But the Isaac Cut teaches us that sometimes the most powerful support comes in the form of ordinary acts offered with extraordinary love, like the difference between a flashy sports car and a reliable vehicle that always starts when you need it.

The beauty of this approach is that it normalizes rather than dramatizes, turning what could be a Very Special Episode moment into something that feels like real life. When someone shares something personal or difficult, they often fear that they'll be treated differently, either with pity (which makes them feel broken), awkwardness (which makes them feel like a burden), or excessive attention to their revelation (which makes them feel like a curiosity rather than a person). The Isaac Cut shows Colin that while his teammates honor his courage in coming out, they're not going to make him feel like an exhibit in a museum or a cause to champion. He's still just Colin, still part of the team, still deserving of the same casual care and friendship he's always received, which is precisely what he needed, even if he couldn't have articulated it beforehand.

Application

The principle behind the Isaac Cut can be applied in countless situations where people around us need support, acceptance, or simply a reminder that they belong, basically, most of human existence, if we're being honest. Here's how to cultivate this approach:

1. **Look for Practical Needs:** When someone is going through a difficult time or has shared something vulnerable with you, resist the urge to offer grand gestures or perfect words. Instead, observe what practical needs they might have with the attention of a detective solving a case, but without the creepiness.
2. **Choose Intimate but Normal Actions:** The most powerful supportive gestures are those that create closeness while feeling natural and unforced. These actions build connection without making the other person feel like they're being treated as a problem to solve or a cause to support, which is the difference between being helped and being fixed.
3. **Follow Someone Else's Lead:** Like Isaac stepping up as captain in this crucial moment, look for opportunities to model acceptance and support for others in your community. When someone takes a risk by being vulnerable or authentic, your response sets the stage for how others will react, like being the first person to clap at a performance.
4. **Resist the Urge to Over-Talk:** In moments of vulnerability, there's often pressure to say the perfect thing or have a deep conversation about feelings, like we're all supposed to be therapists with ideal timing and infinite wisdom. Sometimes, however, the most supportive response is to offer presence and practical care without making the moment.
5. **Make It About Them, Not You:** The Isaac Cut works because it centers Colin's needs rather than Isaac's desire to be seen as supportive, which is the difference between genuine care and performance art. When offering help, focus on what would genuinely serve the other person rather than what would make you feel good about helping.

Takeaway

The Isaac Cut teaches us that love is often spelled H-E-L-P, and the most profound support frequently comes wrapped in the most ordinary packages, like receiving precisely what you need most unexpectedly. In a world that often emphasizes dramatic gestures and perfect words (thanks, romantic comedies), Isaac reminds us that sometimes the most powerful way to show someone they belong is to treat them exactly like they always have, with care, presence, and practical service, but maybe with slightly better hair afterward.

This approach to support is compelling because it doesn't require special training, perfect emotional intelligence, or exceptional resources; basically, it's accessible to anyone who has functioning hands and a functioning heart. Anyone can offer to help with something practical. Anyone can choose presence over avoidance when someone shares something vulnerable (though avoidance is definitely easier, which is why it's so common). Anyone can model acceptance through everyday, caring actions, rather than waiting for someone else to write the script for how these situations should unfold.

The Isaac Cut also reveals something beautiful about community and belonging that's often lost in our individualistic culture. Colin's acceptance doesn't come through tolerance or charity, words that imply he's being granted something he doesn't quite deserve, but through continued membership in the ordinary rhythms of friendship and care. He belongs not because his teammates have decided to be nice to him despite his sexuality (like he's a charity case), but because his sexuality is simply one more thing they know about him, like his position on the field, his taste in music, or his preference for certain types of biscuits. It's information, not a verdict.

This scene reminds us that creating inclusive, supportive communities isn't always about having difficult conversations or implementing complex policies (though those things can be important too). Sometimes it's about individuals choosing to respond to vulnerability with simple kindness, to meet authenticity with acceptance, and to offer practical love in moments when people most need to know they're not alone. It's grassroots acceptance, built one small gesture at a time.

The next time someone in your life takes the risk of being vulnerable or authentic, remember the Isaac Cut and resist the urge to make it more complicated than it needs to be. Ask yourself: "What's the simplest, most practical way I can show this person they belong?" The answer probably won't involve grand gestures or perfect speeches (which are overrated anyway).

When we learn to meet vulnerability with practical love and respond to courage with ordinary care, we create the kind of communities where people can be fully themselves while knowing they're fully supported.

Lesson #20:
It Will All Work Out

The Example:

Ted's quote: *"It may not work out how you think it will or how you hope it does. But believe me, it will all work out."*

--- Ted Lasso (Season 2, Episode 8: "Man City")

This profound piece of wisdom comes at one of the most pivotal moments in Ted Lasso, right after Richmond's devastating 5-0 loss to Manchester City in the FA Cup semifinal. The team is shattered, the fans are devastated, and even Ted's relentless optimism has taken a beating that would make a punching bag file for workers' compensation. Yet in this moment of complete defeat, Ted delivers one of his most important life lessons, like finding a diamond in a pile of really disappointing football statistics.

Context

The context makes this quote even more powerful.

- Ted Lasso delivers this line during a difficult time for the team and for individual characters, notably after a heavy defeat by Manchester City.
- The message is intended to reassure, acknowledging uncertainty and disappointment but emphasizing hope and perseverance.
- The quote comes as several team members, including Jamie Tartt and Coach Beard, are dealing with setbacks both on and off the field.

- Ted's words are meant to encourage belief in a positive outcome, even when things are unclear or plans go awry.
- This moment highlights Ted's optimistic philosophy: offering comfort in adversity, reinforcing belief in resilience and eventual success.
- The quote has become emblematic of the show's ethos about support, trust, and remaining hopeful despite circumstances.

Yet Ted doesn't retreat into bitterness or defensive justification. Instead, he offers this beautifully paradoxical wisdom: life rarely unfolds according to our plans or even our hopes, but somehow—mysteriously, frustratingly, amazingly—it tends to work out in ways we never could have imagined. It's like GPS recalculating your route when you miss a turn, except the destination is happiness and fulfillment instead of the nearest Starbucks.

Throughout the series, we see this philosophy play out in countless ways, like watching a master class in cosmic irony with a surprisingly uplifting ending. Rebecca's revenge plot against Ted completely backfires and ends up healing her own wounds while creating genuine friendship. Roy's forced retirement from playing leads him to discover he's actually brilliant at coaching and commentary (who knew that all that anger could be channeled into useful feedback?). Jamie's humiliation and exile from Richmond ultimately become the catalyst for his personal growth and return as a better person and player.

Ted's quote acknowledges that disappointment and deviation from our plans are inevitable parts of life, but it also suggests that there's a larger pattern at work, one that's often invisible when we're in the middle of the struggle but becomes clear when we look back. It's like being inside a jigsaw puzzle and not realizing you're part of a beautiful picture until someone shows you the box.

The Art of Cosmic Redirection

What makes Ted's philosophy so compelling is how it plays out throughout the entire series, like watching a very slow, very emotional domino effect where each falling piece somehow makes the next one stronger. Take Rebecca's whole arc, which starts with her hiring Ted, specifically hoping he'll fail spectacularly. Basically, she wants him to be the coaching equivalent of a reality TV disaster. She plans to use his incompetence as revenge against her ex-husband Rupert, who left her for a younger woman with all the emotional maturity of a particularly selfish teenager.

But life had different plans for Rebecca, the kind of plot twist that would make even the most creative screenwriter say, "That's too convenient." Instead of watching Ted fail, she ends up witnessing his genuine kindness, his ability to see the best in people, and his knack for creating the kind of supportive environment she never knew she needed. Her revenge plot becomes her healing journey, like accidentally signing up for therapy when you thought you were joining a gym that specialized in emotional destruction.

The same pattern repeats with Jamie, whose journey is essentially a master class in how what appears to be a disaster can actually be exactly what someone needs, even if they would never voluntarily sign up for it. Getting kicked off Richmond and sent to Manchester City seems like the ultimate success—more money, better team, higher profile. But it ultimately exposes the hollowness of his previous approach to life and sets up the circumstances that force him to confront his relationship with his abusive father and his own need for genuine connection rather than just validation.

Even Roy's career-ending injury, which initially devastates him like discovering that your favorite restaurant has permanently closed, becomes the gateway to discovering new aspects of himself. His transition from legendary player to struggling retiree to successful coach and commentator demonstrates how sometimes we must lose our identity to find our purpose. Like being forced to clean out your closet and discovering clothes you forgot you owned that actually look better on you now.

Explanation

Ted's philosophy about things working out touches on one of the most challenging aspects of human existence: how to maintain hope and resilience when life refuses to follow our carefully laid plans, which apparently have about as much influence on reality as a strongly worded letter to the weather.

The phrase "it will all work out" might sound like empty optimism, the kind of thing people say when they can't think of anything actually helpful, like telling someone with a broken leg to "walk it off." But Ted's version is more nuanced than simple positive thinking. He's not promising that everything will turn out exactly as we want it to—in fact, he explicitly acknowledges that it probably won't. Instead, he's suggesting that there's a larger pattern of growth, learning, and ultimately meaningful resolution that often emerges from our struggles, even when we can't see it in the moment.

The key insight in Ted's philosophy is the distinction between our short-term preferences and our long-term well-being. What we think we want in the moment, to avoid all difficulty, to have everything go according to plan, never to face rejection or failure, might actually prevent us from becoming the people we're capable of being or finding the relationships and opportunities that will ultimately bring us the most fulfillment.

Real-World Working Out

Throughout Ted Lasso, we see character after character discover that their lowest moments become the foundation for their highest growth, like watching people accidentally dig wells while they thought they were just digging holes. Nate's transformation from an invisible kit man to assistant coach occurs precisely because Ted's unconventional approach creates space for overlooked talent to emerge, something that would never have happened under a traditional, hierarchical coaching structure.

Dr. Sharon's introduction to the team comes through Ted's panic attacks, which initially seem like a professional disaster and personal failure. But her presence ends up helping not just Ted but multiple team members address their own psychological challenges, creating a culture where mental health is treated as seriously as physical fitness. Ted's apparent weakness becomes the team's collective strength, like accidentally discovering that your biggest insecurity is your superpower.

Even the team's relegation at the end of Season 1, which feels like the ultimate failure, creates the conditions necessary for genuine team building and character development. Without the pressure of Premier League expectations, the players can focus on becoming better people and teammates, which ultimately makes them better players. It's like having to repeat a grade in school and discovering that the second time through, you understand the material instead of just memorizing it for tests.

The show repeatedly demonstrates that what looks like a detour is often actually the main road, just one that we wouldn't have chosen if we were in charge of the navigation system. Rebecca's divorce, which initially devastates her, ultimately frees her to discover who she is outside of her marriage and to build the kind of meaningful relationships she never had access to while trying to be the perfect corporate wife.

Application

Implementing Ted's "it will all work out" philosophy requires both practical strategies and a fundamental shift in how we relate to uncertainty and disappointment, basically, learning to surf instead of trying to control the waves, which is both more fun and more effective in the long run. Here's how to cultivate this approach without becoming someone who passively accepts whatever happens:

1. **Distinguish Between Effort and Outcome:** Focus your energy on what you can control: your preparation, your attitude, your response to challenges, while holding outcomes more lightly.
2. **Develop Patience with Process:** Accept that "working out" often happens on a timeline that's longer than your patience or shorter than your expectations.
3. **Build Resilience Skills:** Since we can't control outcomes, focus on building your capacity to handle whatever comes. This might include developing emotional regulation skills, building strong support networks, maintaining physical health habits that help you cope with stress, and cultivating practices

(meditation, journaling, creative pursuits) that help you process difficulty and maintain perspective.

Takeaway

Ted's wisdom about things working out offers a profound alternative to both anxiety-inducing attempts to control everything and passive resignation to whatever happens. It's a middle path that combines active engagement with humble acceptance, effort with surrender, hope with realism. Essentially, it's like being a skilled improviser who comes prepared but remains open to whatever the scene demands.

The beauty of Ted's approach is that it makes you simultaneously more ambitious and more relaxed, more engaged and more accepting. You can pursue your dreams with full commitment while holding them lightly enough that you won't be destroyed if they don't unfold exactly as expected. You can care deeply about outcomes while not being enslaved by them. Perhaps most importantly, this philosophy transforms your relationship with failure and setbacks. Instead of seeing them as evidence that you're doomed or that life is fundamentally unfair, you can learn to see them as part of a larger process of growth, learning, and ultimately meaningful resolution. Every character in Ted Lasso who learns to trust this process ends up in a better place than they could have imagined when they were trying to control every detail of their journey.

The next time you find yourself frustrated because life isn't going as planned, remember Ted's gentle wisdom.

Your story is still being written, and the best chapters might be the ones you never saw coming, which is either terrifying or exhilarating, depending on whether you choose to trust the process or fight it every step of the way.

Lesson #21:
The Gut-Heart Check-In

The Example:

> Ted's quote: "*Just listen to your gut, and on the way down to your gut, check in with your heart. Between those two things, they'll let you know what's what.*"
>
> --- Ted Lasso (Season 1, Episode 3: "Trent Crimm: The Independent"

This piece of folksy wisdom comes during Ted's conversation with Trent Crimm, the journalist who's trying to understand what makes this American coach tick (and probably wondering if he's dealing with a genius or someone who just watched too many inspirational sports movies).

Context

Here is the context for Ted saying this profound statement.

- Ted Lasso says this line in conversation, offering advice about making decisions during moments of uncertainty or doubt.
- The quote reflects his blend of homespun wisdom and support, combining both instinct ("gut") and emotion ("heart") as essential guides.
- Season 1, Episode 3 features journalist Trent Crimm profiling Ted and attempting to understand his unconventional coaching style.

- Ted uses this line to encourage others to trust their instincts and feelings, instead of overanalyzing every situation, which is central to his approach with the team.
- This quote is emblematic of Ted's philosophy: honest self-reflection leads to better choices, and intuition combined with compassion is the best guide.
- The advice is delivered in a supportive, nonjudgmental way, making it a memorable piece of wisdom from the series.

What makes this quote so brilliant is how it acknowledges that we have multiple internal guidance systems, our gut instincts and our emotional wisdom, and suggests that the best decisions come from consulting both, like getting a second opinion, but from organs that actually live inside you. Ted isn't advocating for purely emotional decision-making, nor is he suggesting we ignore our emotions in favor of pure logic.

Instead, he's proposing a two-step internal consultation process that's both practical and meaningful. First, trust your gut: that mysterious yet surprisingly accurate internal alarm system that somehow knows when something's right or wrong before your brain has finished processing all the data. Then, as you access that gut wisdom, pause and check in with your heart: that emotional intelligence center that understands what you truly care about, what aligns with your values, and what will ultimately bring meaning and fulfillment rather than just temporary satisfaction.

Throughout the series, we see Ted consistently apply this philosophy, often with results that seem almost magical but are actually just the product of someone who's learned to trust his internal guidance system. When he decides to bench Roy Kent despite the potential backlash, his gut tells him it's the right tactical decision while his heart confirms it's also the compassionate choice for Roy's long-term well-being. When he chooses to forgive Rebecca after discovering her sabotage, his gut recognizes her genuine remorse while his heart understands that forgiveness serves everyone involved.

The beauty of Ted's approach lies in its combination of mysticism and practicality. It acknowledges that we have access to wisdom that can't be found in spreadsheets or strategy guides, while also providing a concrete framework for accessing that wisdom when we need it most.

Real-World Gut-Heart Navigation

Throughout, we see characters who get into trouble when they ignore either their gut instincts or their heart's wisdom and find success when they learn to integrate both sources of guidance. Nate's villainous arc in Season 2 occurs partly because he stops trusting his gut feelings about who he wants to be and starts making decisions that are disconnected from his heart, driven by ego and resentment. Basically, he becomes so focused on external validation that he loses touch with his internal compass entirely.

Rebecca's transformation from vengeful owner to genuine team supporter occurs as she learns to listen to both her gut (which tells her that Ted is genuinely good despite her plans to use him) and her heart (which recognizes that her desire for revenge is ultimately making her miserable). Her decision to come clean about her sabotage comes from a gut feeling that honesty is necessary and a heart understanding that authentic relationships require vulnerability.

Roy's journey from angry, retiring player to fulfilled coach happens when he starts trusting his gut about what brings him energy (working with younger players) and checking with his heart about what gives his life meaning (helping others achieve their potential). His initial resistance to coaching comes from ignoring both signals in favor of what he thinks he "should" do based on external expectations.

Even Jamie's redemption arc involves learning to distinguish between gut feelings (which tell him when he's being authentic versus performing) and heart wisdom (which guides him toward connections that are genuine rather than just ego-boosting). His worst decisions come when he's disconnected from both sources of internal guidance, relying instead on his father's toxic programming or media attention.

Explanation

Ted's gut-heart check-in philosophy addresses one of the most challenging aspects of modern decision-making: how to navigate choices in a world that offers endless information but limited wisdom, countless options but unclear guidance about which ones actually serve our wellbeing. We live in an era of decision fatigue, where we're constantly bombarded with data, opinions, and analysis, but often feel more confused rather than more confident about essential life choices.

The traditional Western approach to decision-making tends to privilege rational analysis. We make pro-and-cons lists, conduct cost-benefit analyses, and try to optimize outcomes based on measurable criteria. This analytical approach has obvious value and works well for certain types of decisions (like calculating mortgage payments or choosing insurance plans), but it can fall short when dealing with complex human situations that involve values, relationships, and long-term fulfillment rather than just immediate optimization.

Ted's approach suggests that we have access to other forms of intelligence that can complement and inform our rational analysis, forms of wisdom that are faster than conscious thought but often more accurate than pure logic when it comes to understanding people, situations, and our own authentic needs and desires. The gut-heart check-in isn't about replacing analytical thinking but about creating a more complete decision-making process that includes all available sources of information.

The genius of Ted's sequence—gut first, then heart—reflects an understanding that these two guidance systems work best when they inform each other rather than competing for control. Your gut gives you rapid information about immediate safety and authenticity, while your heart provides slower but deeper insight about meaning, values, and long-term consequences. Together, they create a more complete picture than either could provide alone.

Application

Learning to use Ted's gut-heart check-in effectively requires practice and patience, especially if you've been conditioned to ignore or discount these internal guidance systems in favor of purely rational approaches or external validation. Here's how to develop and refine this internal navigation system:

1. **Develop Gut Awareness:** Start paying attention to physical sensations that accompany different situations and decisions. Notice what happens in your stomach, chest, or shoulders when you're around different people or considering various options. Then wait quietly for physical sensations rather than mental analysis.

2. **Learn Heart Language:** Your heart's wisdom often speaks through emotions, values, and a sense of meaning rather than logic or strategy. Notice the difference between choices that excite your ego ("this will make me look successful") versus choices that resonate with your heart ("this feels meaningful and authentic").

3. **Practice the Two-Step Process:** Before important decisions, literally follow Ted's sequence.

4. **Distinguish Internal Voices:** Learn to recognize the difference between gut-heart wisdom and other internal voices like anxiety, ego, or old programming. Gut feelings tend to be calm and certain even when they're warning you about something, while anxiety is usually frantic and repetitive. Heart wisdom feels expansive and connected to your values, while ego tends to focus on image, comparison, or immediate gratification.

Takeaway

Ted's gut-heart check-in philosophy offers a practical framework for accessing forms of wisdom that complement rational analysis but are often overlooked in our data-driven culture. This approach doesn't replace careful thinking or consultation with others, but it adds valuable sources of information that can guide us toward

sions that are not only smart but also authentic, sustainable, and aligned with our deepest values and needs.

The beauty of this internal guidance system is that it's always available, doesn't require external validation or approval, and tends to become more accurate with practice and attention. While your gut and heart won't always steer you away from difficulty or guarantee easy outcomes, they will generally guide you toward choices that serve your long-term well-being and authentic self-expression rather than just short-term optimization or social expectations. Perhaps most importantly, learning to trust your gut-heart wisdom builds confidence in your ability to navigate life's complexities without needing perfect information or external permission to make important choices. When you know you have access to internal guidance that's both rapid and wise, you can move through uncertainty with greater courage and clarity.

Next time you're facing a tough decision, remember Ted's simple but profound advice. Take a moment to listen to your gut: what does your body tell you about this situation? Then check in with your heart: what choice aligns with your deepest values and authentic self? Between these two internal guides, you'll often find the clarity you need to move forward with confidence.

After all, as Ted demonstrates throughout his journey, the most important navigation happens not through external maps but through internal wisdom, and the best decisions come from leaders who know how to consult both their instincts and their values before charting their course.

Your gut and heart are always available for consultation; you need to remember to ask them what they think before making important decisions.

Lesson #22:
Never Give Up on People

The Example:

Ted's quote: *"Isn't the idea of 'never give up' one of them things we always talk about in sports? And shouldn't that apply to people too?"*

--- Ted Lasso (Season 2, Episode 2:

This seemingly simple question comes during one of Season 3's most emotionally complex moments, when Ted is grappling with whether to continue believing in people who have disappointed him, specifically Nathan Shelley. The context makes Ted's words even more powerful. He's speaking to someone about Nate, who has not only left Richmond for their rival, West Ham, but has also publicly humiliated Ted in the process, essentially becoming the football equivalent of a trusted friend who reveals all your embarrassing secrets to your worst enemy.

Context
Here is the broader context for this quote and belief.

- The quote is spoken by Ted Lasso in Season 2, Episode 2, reflecting his belief that the sports mantra of "never give up" should apply to how people support and treat one another in daily life.
- Ted says these words to his soccer team, AFC Richmond, using the value of perseverance in sports as a bridge to encourage empathy, understanding, and second chances outside of athletic competition.

> The moment occurs as Ted is motivating his team through challenges both on and off the field, making the point that the determination we admire in athletes should also be shown towards those experiencing personal adversity.

- The quote exemplifies Ted Lasso's leadership style, which combines competitive sportsmanship with kindness and a human-centered approach to teamwork and relationships.
- Ted's message inspires both his fictional team and viewers to persist through hardships and treat others compassionately, no matter the circumstances.

Yet, in his characteristic way of finding universal principles in specific situations, Ted takes a step back and asks a profound question that cuts to the heart of what it means to be human. In sports, "never give up" is practically a sacred commandment. We celebrate athletes who return from injuries, teams that overcome seemingly impossible odds, and competitors who refuse to quit, even when the scoreboard appears hopeless. We make movies about these stories, write books about perseverance, and teach children that giving up is the only real failure.

However, when it comes to people — the actual humans in our lives who struggle, make mistakes, and sometimes let us down spectacularly —we often abandon this principle faster than fans leaving a stadium during a blowout loss. We write people off after their first major mistake, decide they're "irredeemable" after their second, and create elaborate justifications for why this particular person is different, why they don't deserve the same patience we'd show a struggling athlete or failing sports team.

Ted's question exposes this inconsistency with the gentle precision of a philosophical surgeon. If we believe in never giving up on comebacks, second chances, and the possibility of redemption in sports, why wouldn't we extend the same faith to the people around us? If we can cheer for a team that's lost ten games in a row because we believe they might turn things around, why can't we maintain hope for a friend, colleague, or family member who's going through their own losing streak?

Throughout the series, we see Ted consistently apply this "never give up on people" philosophy, often with results that seem miraculous but are actually just the natural outcome of persistent belief in human potential. He never gives up on Jamie, even when Jamie is at his most selfish and destructive. He doesn't abandon Roy when Roy is drowning in post-retirement bitterness. He continues to see the good in Rebecca even while she's actively sabotaging his efforts. And yes, even with Nate's betrayal hanging over everything, Ted still can't quite bring himself to write off the person who was once like a son to him.

Here's how Ted's "never give up on people" philosophy plays out:

- Ted consistently sees potential in people that others have dismissed or overlooked
- He maintains faith in people's capacity for growth even when they repeatedly disappoint him
- His approach treats mistakes and failures as temporary setbacks rather than permanent character verdicts
- He creates environments where people feel safe to change and grow, rather than defensive about their past
- Even when setting boundaries, he does so without closing the door on future redemption
- His persistence with "difficult" people often reveals that their behavior comes from pain rather than malice
- The belief itself becomes a catalyst for positive change in ways that criticism or abandonment cannot achieve

The genius of Ted's approach is that it recognizes something profound about human nature: people often become what we consistently believe them capable of becoming, and our faith in their potential can be the difference between their redemption and their continued spiral into whatever darkness they're fighting..

Explanation

Ted's "never give up on people" philosophy challenges some of our deepest assumptions about human nature, justice, and self-protection. In a culture that often treats people as disposable—where "cancel culture" and "cutting toxic people out of your life"

mon responses to disappointment or conflict—Ted's
ch can seem naive, codependent, or even dangerous. After
on't we need to protect ourselves from people who repeatedly
t us? Isn't there a point where continuing to believe in someone
ecomes enabling their bad behavior?

These are legitimate concerns that the show doesn't ignore. Ted's approach isn't about being a doormat or accepting abuse in the name of unconditional love. Instead, it's about distinguishing between holding people accountable for their actions and writing them off as irredeemable human beings. It's possible to set boundaries, protect yourself, and even end relationships while still maintaining hope for someone's eventual growth and redemption.

This isn't magic. It's about how belief creates opportunities, patience allows for growth, and faith provides the emotional safety necessary for genuine change. When people feel written off or judged as fundamentally flawed, they often retreat into defensiveness or embrace the negative identity they feel has been assigned to them. But when they sense that someone still believes in their potential for goodness, growth, and redemption, it can provide the motivation and courage needed to begin the difficult work of change.

Ted's approach also recognizes that people are complex, contradictory beings who contain multitudes—the capacity for both cruelty and kindness, selfishness and generosity, destruction and creation. The person who betrays you today might become your most loyal ally tomorrow, not because they were pretending before, but because circumstances, growth, and the right kind of support can genuinely transform someone's character and choices.

However, it's important to note that "never giving up on people" doesn't mean accepting harmful behavior or sacrificing your own well-being for others' potential growth. Ted maintains boundaries and makes difficult decisions when necessary. He benches players who aren't performing, addresses behavior that hurts the team, and doesn't pretend that good intentions excuse harmful actions. The difference is that he does these things while still holding space for people's capacity to learn, grow, and become better versions of themselves.

Application

Implementing Ted's "never give up on people" philosophy requires both emotional intelligence and practical wisdom. It's about being hopeful without being naive, patient without being passive, and supportive without being enabling. Here's how to apply this approach while maintaining healthy boundaries and realistic expectations:

1. **Distinguish Between Person and Behavior:** When someone disappoints or hurts you, practice separating your response to their actions from your assessment of their fundamental worth and potential. You can hold someone accountable for harmful behavior while still believing in their capacity for growth and change.

2. **Look for the Pain Behind the Pattern:** Ted consistently recognizes that most destructive behavior comes from unmet needs, unhealed wounds, or fear rather than inherent badness. When someone is acting out, ask yourself what pain, fear, or insecurity might be driving their behavior. This doesn't excuse harmful actions, but it can help you respond with wisdom rather than just reaction. pure punishment or abandonment cannot achieve.

3. **Set Boundaries While Maintaining Hope:** "Never giving up on people" doesn't mean accepting abuse or sacrificing your well-being for others' potential growth. You can protect yourself through boundaries, consequences, and even ending relationships while still hoping for someone's eventual healing and redemption.

4. **Practice Strategic Patience:** Genuine change often takes longer than we'd prefer, and it rarely follows a straight line. People typically make progress, have setbacks, make more progress, and have more setbacks before establishing new patterns.

Takeaway

Ted's "never give up on people" philosophy offers a powerful alternative to our culture's tendency toward quick judgment and permanent cancellation. It recognizes that human beings are complex, capable of both tremendous harm and tremendous growth, and that our faith in people's potential can be a catalyst for positive change in ways that criticism or abandonment rarely achieve.

The power of never giving up on people lies not just in what it does for them, but in what it does for us. When we maintain hope for others' growth and potential, we stay connected to our own capacity for compassion, growth, and resilience. We become the kind of people who create environments where positive change is possible, rather than spaces where people feel trapped in their worst moments and behaviors.

Perhaps most importantly, this philosophy recognizes that we all need someone to believe in our capacity for growth, especially during our worst moments. The grace we extend to others during their struggles is often the same grace we'll need when we face our own challenges and mistakes. In sports and in life, the game isn't over until it's over, and people deserve the same benefit of the doubt we'd want for ourselves when we're struggling to find our way back to our best selves.

The next time someone in your life disappoints you or seems to be heading down a destructive path, remember Ted's question: if we believe in never giving up in sports, shouldn't that apply to people too?

Lesson #23:
Love Gets You Through

The Example:

> Ted's quote: "*I think that if you care about someone and you got a little love in your heart, there ain't nothing you can't get through together.*"
>
> --- Ted Lasso (Season 1, Episode 4: "For the Children")

This deceptively simple statement comes during one of Ted's most vulnerable moments in Season 1, when he's grappling with his own marital struggles while trying to help his players navigate their personal challenges. The episode title "For the Children" is significant here, as Ted is essentially talking about approaching all relationships—romantic, familial, professional, and platonic—with the same protective, nurturing instinct we naturally feel toward children who are struggling.

Context
Here is the context for the quote, spoken by Ted Lasso in Season 1, Episode 4: "For the Children".

- Ted delivers this line as part of his ongoing effort to inspire and build trust among those around him, showing optimism and the power of support during challenging times.
- The primary audience in the episode is Rebecca and the wider AFC Richmond community, but the message is universally relevant, directed at anyone facing adversity and in need of encouragement.

- The purpose of the quote is to highlight the importance of human connection, emphasizing that love and care for one another are essential for overcoming difficulties together.
- Ted Lasso, as the person delivering the quote, uses it to reinforce his leadership philosophy: cultivating kindness, fostering teamwork, and reminding everyone that unity and empathy make hardships more bearable.

The context makes Ted's words even more poignant. He's speaking from a place of personal pain, dealing with the slow dissolution of his own marriage despite his best efforts to maintain love and connection across an ocean. Yet rather than becoming cynical about relationships or love's power to solve problems, Ted doubles down on his fundamental belief that care and love are the ultimate problem-solving tools, not because they magically make difficulties disappear, but because they provide the foundation that makes everything else possible.

What makes this quote so powerful is its radical simplicity in a world that tends to overcomplicate relationship advice. We live in an era of relationship experts, communication workshops, and elaborate therapeutic frameworks, all of which can be valuable. But Ted cuts through all the complexity to identify the essential ingredient that makes all other interventions possible: genuine care and love. Without that foundation, all the techniques and strategies in the world are just sophisticated ways of going through the motions.

Ted isn't being naive about the challenges people face. Throughout the series, we see him deal with divorce, betrayal, mental health struggles, family trauma, and professional setbacks. He's not suggesting that love alone prevents these difficulties or that caring about someone automatically resolves all conflicts. Instead, he's proposing that when people genuinely care about each other, they become capable of weathering storms that would otherwise destroy their connection.

Throughout the series, we see this philosophy play out in countless relationships:

- Ted's care for his players helps them through personal crises that could have derailed their careers and lives.
- Rebecca and Ted's growing friendship survives her initial deception because genuine care develops between them.
- Roy and Keeley's relationship weathers major challenges because their fundamental care for each other remains strong.
- The team bonds strengthen not because they avoid conflict, but because their care for each other helps them work through disagreements.
- Even Ted's divorce, while painful, unfolds with more grace because he and Michelle maintain genuine care for each other despite their incompatibility.
- Jamie's transformation happens partly because he experiences genuine care from teammates for the first time in his life.

Ted's insight recognizes that love isn't just an emotion; it's a commitment to seeing challenges as "us versus the problem" rather than "me versus you." When people genuinely care about each other, they naturally approach difficulties as partners seeking solutions rather than adversaries defending positions.

The Limits and Power of Love

Ted's philosophy doesn't claim that love can prevent all problems or guarantee specific outcomes. The show is refreshingly honest about the fact that sometimes caring deeply about someone isn't enough to save a relationship or solve every difficulty. Ted's marriage ends despite his love for Michelle and Henry. Nate betrays Ted despite years of genuine care and mentorship. Some players leave the team despite Ted's investment in their growth and well-being.

But what Ted's approach consistently demonstrates is that love and care maximize the chances of positive outcomes and minimize the damage when relationships do end. His divorce is painful but not bitter. Nate's betrayal hurts but doesn't destroy Ted's faith in people. Players who move on do so with gratitude rather than resentment. Love doesn't guarantee the outcomes we want, but it tends to produce the outcomes we can live with and often creates possibilities we never imagined.

The show also illustrates how love and care need to be genuine rather than manipulative or conditional. Ted's care for people isn't strategic. He doesn't invest in relationships because he expects specific returns. His care is simply an expression of his fundamental belief in people's worth and potential. This authenticity is what makes his approach so effective; people can sense when someone genuinely cares about them versus when someone is caring as a technique to achieve specific results.

Explanation

Ted's philosophy about love getting you through anything challenges both cynical and overly romantic views of relationships. Against cynicism, it insists that love and care are real forces that can overcome significant obstacles and create positive change in people's lives. Against naive romanticism, it acknowledges that love doesn't eliminate difficulties but rather provides the foundation for working through them constructively.

The key insight in Ted's approach is understanding love and care as active choices rather than just feelings. While emotions of love can be unpredictable and temporary, the decision to care about someone's well-being can be maintained even during difficult periods when warm feelings might be absent. This distinction is crucial because it means that the love Ted is talking about isn't dependent on chemistry, compatibility, or even mutual affection. It's a commitment to seeking the best outcome for everyone involved. This approach transforms how we think about conflict and difficulty in relationships. Instead of seeing problems as evidence that love is insufficient or relationships are doomed, we can learn to see them as normal challenges that require the application of love and care to resolve. The question becomes not "Is this relationship worth saving?" but "How can we apply our care for each other to work through this specific difficulty?"

Ted's philosophy also recognizes that love and care are often more powerful than we realize because they tap into our deepest human needs for connection, security, and belonging. When people feel genuinely cared for, they often discover reserves of strength, wisdom, and resilience they didn't know they possessed. Love doesn't just help us tolerate difficulties; it often helps us transcend them and grow through them in ways that make us stronger individually and collectively.

However, it's important to note that Ted's approach doesn't mean accepting abuse, enabling destructive behavior, or sacrificing personal well-being in the name of love. Throughout the series, we see Ted maintain boundaries, hold people accountable, and make difficult decisions when necessary. The love he advocates for is healthy love that seeks the genuine well-being of all parties, not codependent love that enables harm or dysfunction.

Application

Implementing Ted's "love gets you through anything" philosophy requires both emotional generosity and practical wisdom. Here's how to apply this approach while maintaining healthy boundaries and realistic expectations:

1. **Lead with Genuine Care:** In difficult conversations or challenging relationships, start by reminding yourself of your genuine care for the other person's well-being. This doesn't mean agreeing with everything they do or enabling harmful behavior, but it does mean approaching the situation with their best interests at heart alongside your own.

2. **Make Care Visible:** People can't rely on love and care they don't feel or recognize. Find ways to demonstrate your care that the other person can actually perceive and appreciate. That demonstrate his investment in their well-being.

3. **Approach Problems as Partners:** When facing difficulties with someone you care about, frame challenges as "us versus the problem" rather than "me versus you." This shift in perspective naturally leads to collaborative problem-solving rather than adversarial conflict.

4

4. **Balance Care with Boundaries:** Genuine care sometimes requires setting limits, saying no, or allowing people to experience natural consequences of their choices. Learn to distinguish between supporting someone and rescuing them from the growth opportunities that challenges can provide.

Takeaway

Ted's belief that love and care can get you through anything together offers a powerful framework for navigating the inevitable challenges of human relationships. This isn't naive optimism about love conquering all, but rather a practical recognition that genuine care creates the foundation necessary for all other problem-solving efforts to be effective.

The power of this approach lies not in its ability to prevent difficulties but in its capacity to transform how we navigate them. When people feel genuinely cared for, they become more honest, more resilient, more creative in finding solutions, and more willing to do the hard work that growth and change require. Love doesn't eliminate the need for communication skills, boundaries, professional help, or other practical interventions. It makes all of these more likely to succeed.

Perhaps most importantly, Ted's philosophy recognizes that the act of caring deeply for others also transforms us. When we approach relationships and challenges with genuine love and care, we become more patient, more wise, more resilient, and more capable of creating the kinds of connections that sustain us through life's inevitable difficulties.

The next time you're facing a significant challenge in a relationship that matters to you, remember Ted's simple but profound wisdom. Ask yourself: "How can I approach this situation with genuine care for both of us?

Lesson #24:
Don't Fight Back. Fight Forward

The Example:

Ola's quote: "Don't fight back. Fight forward."

--- Ola Obisanya (Season 3, Episode 6: "Sunflowers")

In one of the show's most quietly powerful moments, Sam Obisanya's father, Ola, delivers this profound piece of guidance that transforms how we think about responding to adversity. The scene occurs during a deeply personal conversation between father and son, as Sam grapples with the racist vandalism of his restaurant and the broader challenges of being a young African man trying to make his mark in England.

Context
- Sam's Nigerian restaurant has been vandalized with racist graffiti, devastating him personally and professionally.
- The attack represents broader tensions about Sam's activism and visibility as a young African man in England.
- Sam is struggling with anger, hurt, and the natural desire for retaliation against those who attacked his dream.
- Ola arrives to support his son during this crisis, bringing fatherly wisdom from his own experiences with discrimination.
- The conversation occurs in the damaged restaurant, surrounded by the physical evidence of hatred and ignorance.

- Sam is at a crossroads between letting anger consume him and finding a constructive path forward.
- Ola's advice comes from years of experience navigating prejudice and understanding the most effective forms of resistance.

Sam is understandably angry and hurt, like someone who's just discovered that their favorite coffee shop has been replaced by a store that only sells kale smoothies and positive affirmations. His restaurant, a symbol of his heritage, his dreams, and his contribution to his community, has been defaced with hateful messages that probably required more effort to spray-paint than the perpetrators put into their entire education. The natural human response would be to strike back, to meet hatred with hatred, to defend himself by attacking those who attacked him, basically turning the whole situation into a cycle of revenge that would make Shakespeare nod approvingly while also wondering if anyone learned anything from his plays.

But Ola, drawing from years of wisdom and experience that come from navigating a world that doesn't always welcome people who look like him, offers his son a different path that's both more difficult and more effective than the apparent alternatives.

"Don't fight back. Fight forward."

These five words contain an innovative approach to conflict that goes far beyond football tactics or business strategy, like finding out that the secret to happiness was hiding in your medicine cabinet all along. Still, it's not what you think it is. Ola isn't telling his son to be passive or to accept injustice; that would be like telling someone to smile while being robbed, which helps nobody and probably just confuses the robber. Instead, he's advocating for something much more powerful: channeling that fighting energy not into retaliation, but into progress. Not into looking backward at what was done to you, but forward at what you can build, like being a psychological architect instead of an emotional demolition crew.

The beauty of this moment lies in its cultural specificity and universal applicability, like a perfectly tailored suit that somehow fits everyone who tries it on. Ola speaks as a Nigerian father who understands both the weight of discrimination and the power of perseverance. He's likely faced his own battles, his own moments where the temptation to fight back was overwhelming, like wanting to correct every ignorant comment or respond to every microaggression with the full force of justified anger. Yet he's learned that the most effective resistance isn't reactive—it's creative, constructive, and forward-moving, like being a master chess player who's thinking ten moves ahead while your opponent is still trying to remember how the horsey piece works.

Sam's restaurant represents more than just a business; it's a bridge between cultures, a space where his heritage can flourish while contributing to his adopted community, basically the culinary equivalent of diplomatic relations but with better food and less bureaucracy. When that space is attacked, the instinct is to defend it by attacking back, which makes perfect evolutionary sense but questionable strategic sense in the modern world. But Ola sees the bigger picture: the best defense of what Sam has built is to keep creating, to let his success and contribution speak louder than any retaliation ever could, like drowning out hate speech with the sound of satisfied customers and positive Yelp reviews.

This wisdom echoes throughout history's most effective movements for change, though they probably didn't have Yelp reviews to worry about. The leaders who created lasting progress weren't those who fought back against oppression, but those who fought forward toward a vision of something better. They transformed their pain into purpose, their anger into action, their setbacks into comebacks, basically, they turned their struggles into their superpowers, which sounds like a superhero origin story but is actually just a really good life strategy.

The Philosophy of Forward Motion
What makes Ola's wisdom so profound is how it reframes conflict from a zero-sum game (where someone has to lose for someone else to win) into a creative challenge (where everyone can potentially benefit from better solutions). Throughout Ted Lasso, we see characters who get trapped in fighting-back cycles and those who learn to fight forward, and the results are about as different as

night and day, or as different as a home-cooked meal and whatever they serve at gas stations that technically qualifies as food.

Take Nate's journey in Season 2, which becomes an example of what happens when someone chooses fighting back over fighting forward. When Nate feels overlooked and underappreciated, his response is to attack Ted, the team, and basically everyone who ever believed in him—essentially burning down the village to feel the warmth, which is both literally and metaphorically a terrible heating strategy. Instead of using his hurt as motivation to build something better or prove his worth through positive contributions, he channels his energy into revenge and destruction, which ends up hurting him more than anyone else.

Contrast this with Jamie's approach when he's exiled to Manchester City in Season 1. Initially, he tries the fighting-back approach: being bitter about Richmond, dismissive of his former teammates, and generally acting like someone who got dumped and is now trying to make their ex jealous by dating someone completely inappropriate. But eventually, Jamie learns to fight forward by focusing on becoming a better player and person, which ultimately leads to his triumphant return and genuine redemption.

Rebecca's entire character arc is a journey from fighting back to fighting forward. She starts the series literally sabotaging Ted and the team as revenge against her ex-husband, which is the relationship equivalent of setting your own house on fire because your neighbor's music is too loud. But as she learns to channel her energy into building something positive, supporting the team, developing genuine friendships, creating the life she actually wants—she becomes happier, more successful, and infinitely more likable than when she was focused on making Rupert suffer.

Explanation

The distinction between fighting back and fighting forward represents one of the most crucial choices we face when confronted with adversity, injustice, or personal attacks. Basically, it's the difference between being a professional victim and being a skilled problem-solver, though neither of those is actually a job you can put on your resume. Both responses require courage and energy, but they lead to fundamentally different outcomes, like taking two different roads that start from the same place but end up in entirely different countries.

Fighting back is reactive, like being a sophisticated pinball that responds to whatever hits it but doesn't get to choose its direction. It's allowing others to set your agenda, to dictate how you spend your time and emotional resources, which is basically giving them remote control access to your life without even getting paid for the privilege. When you fight back, you're essentially saying, "Your actions are so important that I'm going to organize my life around responding to them," which gives your opponents way more power over your daily experience than they probably deserve or even want.

You become defined by what you're against rather than what you're for, which is like introducing yourself at parties by listing everything you hate instead of sharing your interests, technically informative but not exactly magnetic. The energy that could be used to create, build, and progress gets consumed in battles that often leave everyone diminished, like participating in a food fight where everybody ends up hungry and covered in mashed potatoes.

Fighting forward, on the other hand, is a proactive approach. It acknowledges the hurt, recognizes the injustice, but refuses to be derailed by it. It transforms opposition into opportunity, obstacles into stepping stones, and setbacks into comebacks, which sounds like motivational poster material but is actually just good strategic thinking.

This doesn't mean being passive or ignoring genuine threats; sometimes, you do need to deal with immediate dangers or protect yourself from ongoing harm. The key is in the motivation and the focus, like the difference between a defensive reaction and an offensive strategy. Are you fighting primarily to defend your past and punish your opponents, or are you fighting mainly from create your future and advance your cause? It's the difference between playing defense for the entire game and actually trying to score points.

Fighting forward requires a different kind of strength—the discipline to resist the immediate satisfaction of retaliation in favor of the longer-term satisfaction of achievement, which is like choosing to eat vegetables instead of cake for dessert, except the vegetables are actually building your dream life and the cake is just temporary revenge that leaves you with a stomachache and no closer to your goals. It means being secure enough in your own worth that you don't need to diminish others to feel valuable, and being clear enough about your goals that you won't be distracted by every provocation, insult, or attempt to drag you into someone else's drama.

Real-World Fighting Forward

The power of fighting forward lies in its efficiency and effectiveness, as exemplified by discovering that the scenic route is actually faster than the highway and offers better views. Revenge is expensive; it costs time, energy, relationships, and often your own moral standing, like paying premium prices for a product that makes you feel worse about yourself. Progress is an investment that compounds over time. Every step forward makes the next step easier, every achievement opens new possibilities, every success creates momentum for the next, like building a snowball that gets bigger and more powerful as it rolls downhill.

Consider the difference in outcomes: fighting back often leads to cycles of retaliation that can go on indefinitely, consuming enormous resources while producing little positive change, like being trapped in a tennis match where nobody's keeping score but everyone's getting increasingly exhausted and angry. Fighting forward breaks those cycles by refusing to participate in them, by changing the game entirely—it forces opponents to respond to your agenda rather than allowing them to set it, like switching from playing defense to offense and watching the other team scramble to keep up.

Throughout Ted Lasso, we see how fighting forward also has a moral dimension that fighting back often lacks. It's harder to oppose someone who's clearly trying to make things better than it is to oppose someone who's trying to make things worse for you. It's the difference between being the villain in someone else's story and being the hero of your own. Fighting forward builds allies rather than enemies, creates positive momentum rather than destructive spirals, and tends to attract people who want to be part of something constructive rather than just witness something destructive.

Even when Sam faces the restaurant vandalism, his ultimate response isn't to seek out the perpetrators or launch a counter-attack against racist elements in the community. Instead, he uses the incident as motivation to make his restaurant even better, to become more visible in positive ways, and to build stronger connections with people who share his values. The vandals probably expected him to either retreat in fear or escalate into conflict; instead, he does something they couldn't predict or prepare for; he gets better and more successful, which is probably the most frustrating possible response from their perspective.

Application

Implementing the "fight forward" mindset requires both strategic thinking and emotional discipline. Basically, you need to become the CEO of your own emotional responses instead of letting them run the company into the ground through poor management decisions. Here's how to make this shift in various areas of your life:

1. **Identify Your Forward Direction:** Before you can fight forward, you need clarity about what "forward" means for you. What are you trying to build, create, or achieve? What's your vision of progress?

2. **Reframe Obstacles as Information:** When facing criticism, setbacks, or attacks, resist the immediate emotional response and ask: "What can this teach me about how to move forward more effectively. Obstacles often contain valuable data about what you need to address, strengthen, or communicate better as you progress, like having a really rude but surprisingly accurate focus group.

3. **Channel Anger into Action:** Anger is energy, and energy can be directed, like having rocket fuel that you can either use to

blow things up or to launch something amazing into orbit. Instead of letting anger consume you in fantasies of revenge or defensive arguments that accomplish nothing except raising your blood pressure, harness it for productive action. Use the fuel of frustration to work harder on your goals, to build stronger systems, to reach new people, to create something so impressive that your critics have to acknowledge it, even if they don't want to.

4. **Build Rather than Tear Down:** When someone criticizes your work, build better work. When someone questions your capabilities, develop stronger capabilities. When someone attempts to limit your opportunities, create new ones, such as being a one-person construction crew while everyone else is focused on demolition.

5. **Choose Your Battles Strategically:** Fighting forward doesn't mean avoiding all conflicts, but it means choosing them based on whether they advance your cause rather than simply satisfy your emotions, like being a strategic general instead of just someone with really strong opinions and good insult skills.

Remember that fighting forward is often more challenging in the moment because it requires delaying the immediate satisfaction of retaliation, such as choosing to invest your money instead of spending it on something that would bring you immediate gratification. But it's more rewarding in the long term because it actually gets you where you want to go, instead of just making you feel temporarily powerful while keeping you stuck in the same place.

Takeaway

Ola Obisanya's wisdom reminds us that we always have a choice in how we respond to adversity: we can let it pull us backward into cycles of retaliation and resentment that keep us stuck in other people's drama, or we can use it to push us forward toward our goals and values, like using resistance training to build stronger muscles instead of just complaining about how heavy the weights are. Fighting back feels satisfying in the moment, but often keeps us stuck in other people's agendas, like being a really dedicated member of someone else's fan club, except the club is focused on making your life worse. Fighting forward feels harder initially but ultimately leads to freedom, progress, and genuine victory that actually improves your life instead of just making you feel temporarily superior.

The most powerful response to those who try to tear you down isn't to tear them down in return. It's to build something so beautiful, so valuable, so undeniably positive that their attacks become irrelevant, like creating such an amazing life that their criticism sounds like background noise you can't even hear over the sound of your own success. When Sam continues to serve excellent food and create community despite the vandalism, he doesn't just restore his restaurant; he transforms it into something even more meaningful, proving that the best revenge isn't revenge at all; it's a life so well-lived that your enemies become irrelevant to your happiness.

This approach requires a fundamental shift in how we define winning. If winning means making your opponents suffer, then fighting back makes sense, and you'll probably spend most of your time focused on other people's misery instead of your own joy. But if winning means achieving your goals, making progress on what matters to you, and creating positive change in the world, then fighting forward is the only strategy that works consistently and doesn't leave you feeling empty even when you get what you thought you wanted.

The next time someone attacks your work, questions your worth, or tries to hold you back, remember Ola's wisdom and ask yourself: "What would fighting forward look like here? How can I use this challenge as fuel for progress rather than an excuse for retaliation?"

The answer might surprise you with its effectiveness and will definitely leave you feeling better about yourself than any revenge plot could ever accomplish.

Lesson #25:
Leave Well

The Example:
> Ted's guidance: "Leave well"—ending with kindness."
> --- Ted Lasso (Season 3, Episode 12: "So Long, Farewell")

I thought it was fitting to have the concluding lesson be Ted's message: "Leave well." In the series finale of Ted Lasso, as the show prepares to say goodbye to its audiences and Ted prepares to return to Kansas, we witness one of television's most graceful departures. [*Note: It turns out not to be the series conclusion as Season 4 is now being filmed.*]

In any case, at that time, Ted doesn't just leave AFC Richmond; he leaves well, which is significantly more difficult than it sounds and infinitely more important than most people realize. This isn't merely about saying goodbye. It's about how we choose to end the chapters of our lives, the relationships we've built, and the roles we've played, basically turning life transitions into an art form instead of a series of awkward shuffles toward the exit.

Context
- Ted has made the difficult decision to return to Kansas to be closer to his son, Henry, after three transformative seasons.
- The series finale shows Ted preparing to leave AFC Richmond, the team that has become his chosen family.
- Despite professional success and deep relationships in England, Ted prioritizes his role as a father.

- The departure is bittersweet, not driven by failure or conflict, but by competing loyalties and life priorities.
- Ted's goodbye process demonstrates how to end meaningful chapters with grace rather than drama.
- Characters throughout the series have struggled with endings, making Ted's approach a masterclass in closure.
- The scene serves as both Ted's farewell to Richmond and the show's farewell to its audience.

"Leave well" becomes Ted's final gift to both his team and to us as viewers, like receiving a perfectly wrapped present that turns out to contain exactly what you needed but didn't know you were missing. It's a philosophy that encapsulates everything the show has taught us about kindness, emotional honesty, and respect; essentially, it's the culmination of three seasons of wisdom distilled into two words that sound simple but require the emotional equivalent of advanced yoga to actually execute properly.

Throughout the series, we've watched Ted arrive with curiosity and optimism (and an impressive collection of folksy sayings), stay with dedication and care (and plenty of dad jokes), and now, in the show's closing moments, leave with grace and gratitude that would make finishing school instructors proud. He doesn't burn bridges or hold onto resentments about the hardships he's faced, which is remarkable considering he's dealt with everything from divorce to panic attacks to having his coaching methods questioned by people who probably couldn't successfully coach a youth soccer team of golden retrievers. He doesn't diminish the value of his experiences because it's ending and instead demonstrates something profoundly counter-cultural: the art of a beautiful goodbye.

The scene resonates profoundly because it challenges one of life's most difficult transitions. By "challenging," we mean "the kind of thing most people would rather avoid by faking their own death and moving to a small island." Endings are tough, whether it's leaving a job (even one where your boss made you question your will to live), ending a relationship (even when you know it's for the best), moving away from a community (even when the neighbors were questionable), or simply graduating from school (and facing the terrifying prospect of adult responsibilities). We often struggle with how to close the chapters of our lives, like trying to write the perfect ending to a story when you're not entirely sure what the story was about to begin with.

Do we slip away quietly to avoid the pain, like emotional ninjas who disappear into the night, leaving only confusion and unanswered texts? Do we burn it all down in a dramatic exit that would make reality TV producers weep with joy? Do we cling desperately, trying to prevent the inevitable change like someone trying to stop time by covering all the clocks in the house?

Ted offers a fourth choice that's both more challenging and more fulfilling than any of those options: leave well. This involves recognizing what the experience has meant, showing gratitude to the people who shared it with you, offering forgiveness where necessary (even if they haven't earned it), and departing with your integrity and kindness intact, like a professional farewell artist rather than just someone who's awkward at goodbyes. It also means resisting the urge to rewrite history negatively just because something is ending, such as suddenly declaring that your favorite restaurant was terrible just because it's closing, and instead choosing to cherish what was beautiful about the time you shared.

The Richmond Departure

What makes Ted's departure so masterful is how it contrasts with other endings we've seen in the series, creating a beautiful example of how to handle transitions gracefully instead of chaotically. Remember Rebecca's divorce from Rupert, which was practically a masterclass in how **not** to end things: bitter, vindictive, and only aimed at causing maximum damage rather than healing or moving forward? Or Nate's departure to West Ham, which involved betrayal, public humiliation, and burning bridges with the skill of someone who majored in relationship destruction?

Ted's approach is the complete opposite of these dramatic exits. He doesn't leave out of anger, disappointment, or to make a point. He leaves because life circumstances change, and he needs to focus on his relationship with his son, Henry, which is both heartbreaking and completely understandable. His departure isn't about Richmond failing him or him failing Richmond; it's about understanding that sometimes good things end not because they have turned bad, but because other good things deserve attention.

Throughout his final episodes, we see Ted making intentional choices about how to handle his departure. He talks to people directly rather than sending a group text or having someone else deliver the news. He spends time having individual conversations with players, acknowledging their unique contributions and growth. He shows sincere gratitude for what Richmond has given him, even while feeling sad about leaving. Most importantly, he doesn't try to make his departure about himself. He focuses on preparing the team for success without him, like a caring parent who teaches their kids to be independent instead of dependent.

The contrast with other characters' approaches to endings is striking. When Roy initially retired, he became a bitter hermit who seemed to believe that if he couldn't play football, then football itself was meaningless, almost the athletic equivalent of taking his ball and going home, except the ball represented his entire identity. When Jamie left for Manchester City, he acted like Richmond had been holding him back all along, rewriting history to justify his departure rather than acknowledging the genuine relationships and growth he experienced.

Explanation

The idea of leaving well is very different from how many handle endings in our culture, where we often see departures as either horror movie scenes or disappearing acts that would impress magicians. Too often, we treat departures as either traumatic breaks (with door slamming and dramatic statements) or awkward vanishings (the emotional equivalent of ghosting someone, but for entire stages of life). We ghost people to avoid tough talks because explaining why we're leaving feels harder than just vanishing as if we never existed. We create conflict to justify leaving, basically, starting fights so we can storm out confidently instead of admitting we just need to move on. We downplay what we're leaving behind to make the departure easier, like suddenly saying your job was terrible, your friends were annoying, and your apartment was a dump, not because it's true, but because it makes leaving feel less like a loss.

Or we become so focused on what comes next that we fail to properly honor what is concluding, like already mentally decorating your new place before you've finished packing the old one, which is both practically problematic and emotionally unsatisfying.

Leaving well requires emotional intelligence and intentionality, which is essentially the opposite of how most people handle transitions. Typically, they panic, avoid, or hope everything will just work out without genuine effort. It involves being present for the ending, not rushing through it or trying to skip the discomfort, like someone fast-forwarding through the sad parts of movies. It means recognizing both the joys and the challenges of what you're leaving behind, not pretending everything was perfect (which would be dishonest and probably unbelievable) but also not focusing solely on what went wrong (which would be unfair or ultimately destructive).

At its core, leaving well is about gratitude and respect, which seems simple but is actually quite revolutionary in a culture that tends to focus on what's wrong rather than what's been valuable and meaningful. It's about recognizing that every experience, relationship, and role has contributed something to who you are, even if that contribution wasn't always pleasant or obvious at the time. Difficult situations often teach us valuable lessons or help us develop resilience we wouldn't gain otherwise. Relationships that didn't work out perfectly usually contained moments of genuine connection or care that enriched our lives. Jobs we've outgrown likely offered opportunities for growth or introduced us to important people, even if the work became mind-numbing or the boss lacked management skills.

This doesn't mean being dishonest about problems or pretending that endings aren't sometimes necessary because of real issues. Toxic relationships should end, abusive situations should be escaped, and sometimes people really do need to leave environments that are damaging their well-being or stunting their growth. Leaving well isn't about fake positivity or avoiding brutal truths, like pretending everything is fine when it clearly isn't. Instead, it's about holding complexity, acknowledging what was hard while still appreciating what was good, being honest about why you're leaving while still expressing genuine gratitude for what you're taking with you, like being an emotional archaeologist who can sort through the rubble to find the valuable artifacts worth preserving.

The Ripple Effect of Graceful Endings

The practice of leaving well also benefits those you're leaving behind, which is important because how you exit influences not only your own future but also their ability to process the change and move forward positively. When someone departs with grace and appreciation, it helps others view the ending more positively. Instead of feeling abandoned, rejected, or that their time was wasted on the relationship, they can feel honored and grateful for what was shared. It affirms the time and energy they invested, making the experience feel meaningful rather than pointless. It demonstrates emotional maturity and indicates that their connection was genuine and valuable, a gift they carry with them long after you're gone.

Throughout Ted Lasso, we see how Ted's approach to leaving well creates positive ripple effects that go far beyond his own departure. The players don't feel abandoned or betrayed. They feel prepared and appreciated. Rebecca doesn't feel like she wasted three years believing in someone who didn't truly care about Richmond. She feels like she was part of something meaningful that will keep influencing her leadership style. Even characters who initially struggled with Ted's departure, like Roy, eventually come to understand and respect his choice because of how thoughtfully and caring he handled the transition.

Perhaps most importantly, leaving well serves your own emotional health and future relationships, which is crucial because carrying baggage from poorly handled endings is like trying to run a marathon while wearing a backpack full of rocks, technically possible but unnecessarily difficult and ultimately counterproductive. When you leave situations with unresolved anger, burned bridges, or unspoken resentments, you carry that baggage into whatever comes next, like having emotional luggage that never quite fits in the overhead compartment of your new life. But when you take the time to leave well—to express gratitude, offer forgiveness, and depart with kindness—you free yourself to fully embrace new opportunities without being weighed down by the ghosts of poorly handled endings.

Leaving well also preserves opportunities in ways that dramatic exits never can. Relationships that end gracefully can sometimes be renewed later under different circumstances. Perhaps the job you left thoughtfully will want to rehire you someday, or the friend you parted with kindly will be there when you need support years later. Professional connections maintained through thoughtful departures can lead to future opportunities you never could have expected. Communities you leave with respect and appreciation may welcome you back or continue to support you from afar, creating networks of goodwill that last much longer than the original relationship.

Application

Implementing the practice of leaving well requires both preparation and presence. Basically, you need to be both strategic and sincere, which is harder than it sounds but infinitely more rewarding than the alternatives. Here's how to approach endings with Ted's wisdom:

1. **Pause Before You Leave:** When you know an ending is approaching, whether it's a job change, relationship conclusion, or significant life transition, resist the urge to mentally check out early like a student in their last week of school. This is harder than it sounds because once you've decided to leave, your brain wants to start the leaving process immediately, but staying engaged until the end is what separates graceful exits from awkward fade-outs.

2. **Reflect on the Gifts:** Before your departure, take time to genuinely consider what this experience has given you, and by

"genuinely" we mean actually thinking about it, not just going through the motions.

3. **Express Appreciation Specifically:** Generic thank-yous, while nice, don't carry the same impact as specific acknowledgments. It's the difference between saying "you're great" and explaining exactly why someone made a difference in your life. Tell people exactly what their contribution meant to you, with the specificity of someone who actually paid attention and cared enough to remember details.

4. **Address Unfinished Business:** If there are unresolved conflicts or misunderstandings, consider whether it's possible and appropriate to address them before you leave, not because you need to fix everything (some things can't be fixed and that's okay), but because leaving with clarity is usually better than leaving with confusion.

5. **Share Your Learning:** Part of leaving well involves contributing to the success of what you're leaving behind, like being a good predecessor instead of just someone who used to work there. Share insights that might help others, document processes that only you know, introduce connections that might be valuable, or offer to help with the transition in whatever way is appropriate and sustainable. This transforms your departure from a loss into a gift, demonstrating that you care about the organization's or relationship's continued success, even though you won't be part of it.

6. **Create Positive Closure Rituals:** Plan meaningful ways to mark the ending that feel authentic to you and the relationships involved. This might be a lunch with colleagues to share favorite memories, a walk through places that hold significance for you, or writing letters to people who have made a difference. Basically, it's about creating intentional moments of connection and reflection instead of letting endings happen accidentally.

7. **Keep Doors Open Thoughtfully:** Let people know you value the relationship beyond the specific context you're leaving, but be genuine about this, only make offers you actually

intend to keep, because nothing ruins a graceful exit like promising to stay in touch and then disappearing forever.

8. **Plan Your Re-entry:** Consider how you want to engage with this person, place, or community in the future, because leaving well often means you're welcome to return for visits, events, or even a future role.

Remember that leaving well is a skill that gets better with practice, just like any other part of emotional intelligence. However, I wouldn't suggest leaving many situations just to practice. Every time you end something gracefully, you become better at managing transitions and more confident in your ability to handle change while keeping relationships and integrity intact. Plus, you build a reputation as someone trustworthy to handle tough situations with maturity and kindness.

Takeaway

Ted Lasso's final lesson to us, to leave well, is perhaps his most important gift because it's the one we'll use most often throughout our lives, like a really good multitool that turns out to be useful in situations you never anticipated. We will all face countless endings: jobs will conclude, relationships will evolve or come to an end, phases of life will come to a close, and eventually, we'll face our own final departure from this world. How we handle these transitions shapes not only our own experience but also the experience of everyone we touch along the way, creating ripples that extend far beyond what we can see or predict.

Leaving well is an act of love, love for the people we're leaving behind, love for the experiences we've shared, and love for ourselves as we move forward into whatever comes next. It's a recognition that nothing beautiful is ever truly wasted, even when it ends, and that the kindness we show in departing becomes part of the legacy we leave, the memory others carry of us, and the foundation we build for whatever comes next.

In a culture that often treats endings as failures or focuses obsessively on new beginnings while ignoring the importance of conclusions, choosing to leave well is both countercultural and healing. It suggests that completion can be as beautiful as commencement, that goodbyes can be as meaningful as hellos, that the way we end things matters as much as the way we begin them, revolutionary concepts in a world that tends to focus on starts rather than finishes.

Ted's departure from Richmond becomes a masterclass in graceful endings; not because it's easy or painless, clearly, it's difficult for everyone involved, and both characters and viewers shed genuine tears, but because it's intentional, kind, and honoring of what was shared. He doesn't pretend the goodbye isn't hard, but he also doesn't let the difficulty of leaving overshadow the beauty of what was experienced, like being able to appreciate a sunset even though you're sad the day is ending.

The next time you face an ending, whether it is major or minor, chosen or imposed, remember Ted's wisdom and ask yourself: "How can I leave well here? How can I honor what this has meant while gracefully transitioning to what comes next?" The answer to that question will not only make the departure more meaningful for everyone involved but also help you start your next chapter with a clear conscience, an open heart, and the confidence that comes from knowing you can handle life's transitions with grace and kindness.

Ultimately, leaving well isn't just about how we say goodbye. It's about living each day knowing that everything is temporary, every relationship is valuable, and every chance to be kind matters, right up until the final moment when we close one door and open another.

And with this last lesson, I hope to leave you feeling inspired to make your life a little better!

Conclusion:
Choosing Empathy, Practicing Optimism

When the final whistle blows and the stadium empties, we're left not just with the score but with the memory of how the game was played. That is the lasting gift of Ted Lasso. Over three seasons, he showed us that the true measure of a life or a team isn't how many trophies you win, but how you treat people along the way. And as this book has tried to demonstrate, the lessons Ted embodied can carry us well beyond the playing field, shaping our work, our families, our communities, and even how we see ourselves.

At the heart of it all are two deceptively simple commitments: **empathy** and **optimism**. These are the twin threads that tie together every story, every laugh, every heartbreak in *Ted Lasso*. Empathy calls us to see others not as obstacles or opponents, but as fellow travelers, each carrying invisible burdens. Optimism reminds us to believe—not blindly, but stubbornly—that tomorrow can be better than today, that people can change, and that joy can be found even in the struggle

Empathy in Action

Empathy in Ted's world wasn't just soft sentimentality; it was a discipline. When he noticed a player's pain, he didn't dismiss it or mask it with clichés; he engaged, asked questions, and offered the gift of being truly seen. He demonstrated that empathy isn't passive; it involves listening when we'd rather speak, choosing curiosity over judgment, and sometimes holding space for someone's sorrow without rushing to fix it.

In our lives, this practice of empathy can transform classrooms, boardrooms, dinner tables, and locker rooms alike. It's what allows a leader to see potential in an overlooked employee, a parent to notice what lies beneath a child's tantrum, or a friend to hear the pain behind another's silence. Empathy doesn't eliminate conflict, but it changes how we engage with it, making resolution possible without winners and losers. It reminds us that every person we meet carries a story worth hearing.

The Courage of Optimism

Optimism is often misunderstood as naive cheerfulness, but Ted showed it as a form of strength. To hope despite failure, to motivate others when the odds are against you, that takes resilience, not denial. Optimism is what helped Richmond's players imagine a different future from their past, and what allowed a skeptical fan base to find joy again in a team that had long let them down.

In our fractured world, optimism isn't about ignoring pain. It's about insisting that despair won't have the final word. It's about remembering that growth is always possible, that reconciliation can happen, and that even the smallest acts of kindness ripple outward in unpredictable ways. Optimism is the fuel that sustains empathy when cynicism whispers that people don't change.

Lessons That Stay With Us

Each of the 25 lessons in this book has its own texture and flavor, from "Be curious, not judgmental" to "It's the lack of hope that gets you" to the art of leaving well. But together, they tell a bigger story. They remind us that leadership isn't about authority; it's about service. That forgiveness frees both the forgiver and the forgiven. That vulnerability isn't weakness; it's the birthplace of connection.

And finally, that endings are just as important as beginnings. Ted's farewell at Richmond demonstrated what it means to "leave well"—to honor the past, bless the present, and make room for the future. This final lesson is a gift we'll carry with us long after the series fades from memory, because everyone will face goodbyes. How we say them will shape the stories others tell about us.

Carrying the Lessons Forward

As you close this book, I encourage you not just to remember these lessons but to put them into practice. Empathy and optimism only grow stronger through action. Ask yourself: Where can I listen more deeply today? Where can I choose hope when it's easier to give in to cynicism? Where can I create space for others to shine?

You don't need to coach a football team to live like Ted Lasso. You just have to show up for the people in your life with kindness, curiosity, and courage. You only need to believe, not in a slogan on a locker room wall, but in the potential of human goodness, renewed each day through a thousand small choices.

Ted Lasso's world might be fictional, but the change it inspires is real. The lessons last because they're based on timeless truths about who we are and who we can become. If we take them seriously, we might find ourselves not only better leaders, coworkers, parents, or friends, but, as Ted might say with that trademark grin, "better humans."

Made in United States
Orlando, FL
11 October 2025